4-20-71

ALL GOD'S CHILLUN

ALL GOD'S CHILLUN

Meditations on Negro Spirituals

J. Garfield Owens

♪ Abingdon Press • Nashville & New York

ALL GOD'S CHILLUN

Copyright © 1971 by Abingdon Press

ISBN 0-687-01020-9

Library of Congress Catalog Card Number: 79-134257

SET UP, PRINTED, AND BOUND BY THE
PARTHENON PRESS, AT NASHVILLE,
TENNESSEE, UNITED STATES OF AMERICA

To Arthur Lee Hobbs Owens, my wife,
my friend and companion in all seasons,
and
to my many friends of
the Warren United Methodist Church,
whose warm words of encouragement
helped to bring this book into being

Contents

* See editor's note, page 12.

Introduction

The essays on the Negro spirituals which appear in this volume grew out of more than fifteen years' effort to preach the Gospel using some of the profound insights of the Negro slaves. Since these beautiful songs were as native to my early years as the air I breathed, I can safely say that my own spiritual life is, to a great extent, the product of their nourishment.

During my study and meditation upon these noble songs, I have come to recognize that they are more than simply folk songs. There is expressed in them a way of life, a philosophy of life. They represent the unconscious efforts of the Negro slaves to make sense of their shattering life situations. They represent the rare genius with which the slaves distilled the best from their own tradition and way of life and blended it with their newly found Hebrew-Christian tradition. In their songs the slaves tell in words, nuances, and music of their struggles, weariness, loneliness, sorrow, hope, determination, and assurance.

The themes of these songs, in most instances, were lifted directly from the Hebrew-Christian Bible. Someone has rightly said that should all the Bibles be lost and a generation grow up without any knowledge of the Bible, a general outline of the Bible could be found in the study of the great themes of the Negro spirituals.

I have come to the conclusion that many of the great spirituals were God-given songs. They were given to these particular people under their own particular slave circumstances. But, like all truly God-given messages, these songs not only spoke to the hearts of the slaves, but continue to speak most eloquently to our day. In many instances the slave singers sang far more truly about life in general than they ever knew themselves. Thus I have sought to point out some of the obvious and more subtle implications in the spirituals which may not have been evident to the slaves themselves.

It is apparent that the Negro spirituals have ever-increasing meaning and relevance for our times. Our is a day—and happily so—when the young blacks are speaking with great pride about black heritage and black identity. In the great body of Negro spirituals there is a priceless legacy of which we can all be justly proud. Through their songs the slaves made noble contributions to the religious, cultural, artistic, and aesthetic life of America and the world. It is my hope that these comments on the spirituals will call attention anew to the beauty and wonder of these songs. I also hope that I have been able to correct a few errors—which I feel to be serious ones—in some earlier interpretations of the spirituals. There were those who thought there were no traces of hate or bitterness or resentment in the spirituals. This, I am convinced, is a misreading of the message of these songs. One finds in almost all the Negro spirituals— even in the most beautiful and deeply religious—strong elements of resentment, bitterness, revenge, and protest. Much of this expression, of course, was presented in disguised

10

form and almost in code language. I feel that there is no need to try to make angels of the slaves; they were human children of earth, and they made human responses to human situations.

The slaves protested in their songs to the degree to which they felt safe. It should be understood that the great and loud outcries against injustices which are heard today on the part of the children of the slaves are none other than amplifications of the muffled and stifled cries of yesterday which were expressed in the spirituals.

Again there has been a general feeling that the Negro spirituals were predominantly otherworldly. This also I believe to be untrue, unless it means that they sang about a world of freedom as opposed to the world of slavery. The songs of the slaves are deeply encouched in biblical imagery and figures of speech: the promised land, the Jordan, the new Jerusalem, the sweet chariot coming down, etc. But these are basically nothing more than the hardheaded longings of the slaves for the God who would lead them into the land of freedom.

These songs were also pep songs, or morale builders. The slaves would sing with great enthusiasm to the weary travelers among them. They sought to encourage the lonely and to give new spirit to the fainthearted.

Finally, I have sought to have the spirituals speak their message to the slaves and to the times and conditions of the slaves. I have also sought to point out the great and lasting truths which these beautiful songs suggest for our time and for all times.

I have used and found helpful in my study the following

11

books: *The Negro Spiritual Speaks of Life and Death* and *Deep River* by Howard Thurman; *My Songs* by Roland Hayes; and *The Book of American Negro Spirituals* and *The Second Book of Negro Spirituals* by James Weldon Johnson and J. Rosamond Johnson.

* Editor's note: The reader will notice that there is inconsistency in the spelling of some words in the spirituals; for instance, "chillun" and "children." This is because there is no "correct" way to render dialect. The version used in a particular song was usually chosen because the rhyme or rhythm of the song demanded a certain sound or number of syllables. In all cases, the spelling and stanza sequence that seemed to be the best of many in print were chosen.

All God's Chillun
Got a Song

I got a song, you got a song,
  All God's chillun got a song;
When I get to heab'n, goin' to sing a new song,
  Goin' to sing all over God's heab'n.

Heab'n heab'n, ev'rybody talkin' 'bout heab'n ain't
    goin' dere,
Heab'n, heab'n, goin' to shout all over God's heab'n.

I got shoes, you got shoes,
  All God's chillun got shoes;
When I get to heab'n, goin' to put on my shoes,
  Goin' to walk all over God's heab'n.

I got a robe, you got a robe,
  All God's chillun got a robe;
When I get to heab'n, goin' to put on my robe,
  Goin' to shout all over God's heab'n.

I got a harp, you got a harp,
  All God's chillun got a harp;
When I get to heab'n, goin' to take up my harp,
  Goin' to play all over God's heab'n.

He hath put a new song in my mouth.—Psalm 40:3*a*

God . . . who giveth songs in the night.—Job 35:10*b*

I call to remembrance my song in the night.—Psalms 77:6*a*
And they sung as it were a new song before the throne.—
  Revelation 14:13*a*

And white robes were given unto every one of them.—
  Revelation 6:11*a*

*Behold the fowls of the air; for they sow not, neither do
they reap, nor gather into barns; yet your heavenly Father
feedeth them. Are ye not much better than they? . . . Consider the lilies of the field, how they grow; they toil not,
neither do they spin: And yet I say unto you, that even
Solomon in all his glory was not arrayed like one of these.*—
  Matthew 6:26, 28*a*-29

This is one of the truly great spirituals. It expresses the
deep yearnings and the profound hope and assurance of the
slaves. One hears in it the ring of optimism so characteristic
of many of the great spirituals.

We must keep in mind that in many of the spirituals
the slaves dealt with two prevailing themes: protests against
the system of slavery and the deprivations which it inflicted
upon them; and songs to reassure themselves that God was
ever at work on their behalf to bring about their redemption.
In this song both themes are very pronounced and very
beautifully and skillfully interwoven. Let us pause at the
phrase of joyful assurance: "All God's Chillun Got a Song."
Here the slaves are singing out of their own deep experiences.
They know in their hearts that they have a song. For God
had given them a song even in their dark night. This song
represents a true revelation of the bright morning stars
shining out of that dark and shameful night of human

14

slavery; God gave to his children of servitude a song, and they sang their song with melody sublime.

Hear the slaves as they assured each other: "I got a song, you got a song, all God's chillun got a song." No matter where they may be, no matter how dark the night, how heavy the load, or what their outward circumstances may be, God's children surely can be recognized, because they always have a song. They may be robbed of their freedom, left motherless, fatherless, or childless; tossed and driven, beaten and scorned; but no one, nor any conditions, can take away their song. So they still sing on, "We are God's children." Oh, how they do sing on!

One can hear in the slave songs the mourning and groaning of an oppressed people, and yet one can recognize in them also the hopes, yearnings, and determination of invincible spirits. Here in this song of sorrow is expressed a beauty, a tenderness, and a sweetness that are rarely surpassed anywhere. God, according to his mercies, transformed the anguished longings and sorrowful cries of these burdened souls into some of the world's most beautiful and profound music. For all God's children do have a song.

The slaves, dispossessed of everything, denied the privilege of pursuing earthly goods, their labor and toil all going for the enrichment of their masters, would not and could not believe that they were beyond God's loving providence. They contrasted their own condition with that of the master's household. The master's house seemed to have all the earthly goods that made for a happy and meaningful life. The slaves, enclosed in one-room, crowded huts, with ragged clothing, bare feet, and coarse food, would not believe that this would be their plight forever. For God had ordained

15

that all his children should have robes and shoes. So they made known their own beliefs in and claims to God's loving care: "I got shoes, you got shoes, all God's chillun got shoes. . . . I got a robe, you got a robe, all God's chillun got a robe."

Had not Jesus, God's own Son, assured his followers that his heavenly Father, who clothed the lilies of the fields, and who fed the sparrows, would surely meet all of their needs? This blessed promise was extended to them as well. Thus they were assured that God would provide for them. Man's evil design might temporarily deny them their rightful shoes and robes, but they were sure that God's enduring love and power would prevail. Someday, in joy and freedom, each person would put on his robe and shoes. Even if earth should deny me these goods; "When I get to heab'n, goin' to put on my robe, goin' to shout all over God's heab'n."

The slave singers did not find too many reasons for real rejoicing. Very few of the spirituals are genuine songs of praise. However, the singers knew that there should be moments of rejoicing and high praise in their lives as well as in the lives of others. They were aware of the happy events which took place in the master's house. They witnessed the playing of the harps and the glorious and hilarious occasions. They had no special occasion for making merry. They had no harps made of silver or brass; but they did have harps. What instrument can make music as sweet and melodious as the lips of God's children? It has been ordained that all God's children should be able to play their harps, to rejoice, and to enjoy life. If slavery and its conditions should deny us the privilege of playing our

16

earthly harps, we will, in perfect freedom, play our heavenly harps, the slaves so beautifully stated:

> When I git to heab'n, goin' to take up my harp,
>   Goin' to play all over God's heab'n.
> Heab'n, heab'n, ev'rybody talkin' 'bout heab'n ain't
>   goin' dere,
> Heab'n, heab'n . . .

Their deep religious faith assured the slaves that they were candidates for God's Heaven. This hope and certainty of heaven for them were based on their faith in the love and mercy and righteousness of God. Although the ugly and brutal facts of slavery encompassed them, the slaves were certain that somewhere, at God's appointed time, the inequities of life would be erased. "Some day we'll be free, our burdens lighter, our troubles over, and our trials ended" were words of assurance for them. So if need be, they could wait for their assured place in God's heaven.

Somehow they were not so sure that their masters were going to heaven. The Scriptures seemed to suggest that the loveless, the cold of heart, those who mistreated their neighbors or abused the stranger and the homeless just might not get to heaven. The line of the song "Ev'rybody talkin' 'bout heab'n ain't goin' dere" probably referred to their masters.

Fortified with the assurance that God's heaven would be theirs, they could sing with great enthusiasm:

> Oh, I'm gwinter sing all along de way,
>   Oh, I'm gwinter sing all along de way,
> We'll shout o'er all our sorrows, an' sing forever more,
>   With Christ an' all his army, on dat celestial shore.

Swing Low, Sweet Chariot

Swing low, sweet chariot, comin' for to carry me home,
Swing low, sweet chariot, comin' for to carry me home.

I looked over Jordan, an' what did I see, comin' for to carry
me home?
A band of angels comin' after me, comin' for to carry me
home.

If you get dere before I do, comin' for to carry me home,
Tell all my friends I'm comin' too; comin' for to carry me
home.

I'm sometimes up, I'm sometimes down, comin' for to
carry me home,
But still my soul feels heaven bound; comin' for to carry
me home.

*And it came to pass, as they still went on and talked, that
behold, there appeared a chariot of fire and horses of fire,
and parted them both asunder; and Elijah went up by a
whirlwind into heaven.*—II Kings 2:11

*And Elisha prayed and said, Lord, I pray thee, open his
eyes that he may see. And the Lord opened the eyes of the
young man and he saw; and behold, the mountain was full
of horses and chariots of fire round about Elisha.*—
II Kings 6:17

19

The angel of the Lord encampeth round about them that bear him and delivereth them.—Psalm 34:7

For me to live is Christ and to die is gain. But if I live in the flesh, this is the fruit of my labour; yet what I shall choose I wot not. For I am in a strait betwixt two, having a desire to depart, and to be with Christ; which is far better.—
Philippians 1:21-23

"Swing Low, Sweet Chariot" is perhaps the most beautiful of all the Negro spirituals. Its poetic beauty and rich-though-simple images are unsurpassed. In it is reflected the deep, abiding religious faith of the slaves.

Slave poets and singers took their images and pictures straight from the Holy Scriptures. Most of them could not read, yet when they heard a passage of scripture read they never forgot it. For in the scriptures they heard God's rich promises for them.

To the slaves, God, his angels, his chariots, and the heavenly hosts were never far away. The other world was only a breath away from this old world of sorrow and woe. So often disenchanted with this world and its terrible injustices, they longed for the other world where God's ideal justice prevailed. They could sing with joy and expectation: "De udder world is not like dis."

It has been suggested that this beautiful expression "swing low, sweet chariot" came from the heart of some unknown, weary, and broken soul, perhaps while he was working in the fields where the end of the rows came to a river. The river suggested to the tired and troubled soul the spiritual river that separated it from its blessed home of rest and peace. So the weary and sorrowful poet, knowing he was

20

ever surrounded by the heavenly host, could say, "Oh, sometimes my burdens are so hard to bear, my sorrows so heavy, and my troubles so great; I wish the Lord would just send his chariot and carry me on home."

The unknown bards continued their song with this beautiful and almost childlike picture: "I looked over Jordan, and what did I see? A band of angels coming after me." What a beautiful interpretation of the death of God's saints! Death was for them only a coming of God's chariot and angels to carry them home. But the mood of the slaves, like that of any other people, was changeable. Sometimes during a long and bitter night, the candle of their faith burned low, but it never burned out. They sang: "I'm sometimes up and I'm sometimes down, but still my soul feels heaven bound." This expression is heard again and again in many of their songs, and what one among us has not experienced such ups and downs? The miracle of miracles is that men living under such terrible conditions could feel up at all, yet they did. For they knew that even though they were denied their real and rightful home here, man's inhumanity to man could not ultimately thwart God's purpose for his children. They knew in their hearts that God had prepared a home for all.

So moving patiently and hopefully toward that home, they could shout to those who may have outrun them: "If you get dere before I do, tell all my friends I'm comin' too." They knew that when they were at home with God they would be reunited with friends. The system of slavery, without mercy, tore mothers from children, brothers from sisters, friends from friends. What shadow of home they might have had was always threatened by the auction block. But when they went home to be with God, all the broken pieces

21

of the family would be rejoined. Friends would be forever reunited and shattered bonds would be restored. It was because of their unconquerable faith, undying hope, and blessed assurance that they could shout and sing, "Swing low, sweet chariot, coming for to carry me home."

Deep River

Deep river, my home is over Jordan;
Deep river, Lord, I want to cross over into campground.
   Lord, I want to cross over into campground,
   Lord, I want to cross over into campground,
   Lord, I want to cross over into campground.

O don't you want to go to dat Gospel feast,
Dat promised land where all is peace?
   Lord, I want to cross over into campground,
   Lord, I want to cross over into campground,
   Lord, I want to cross over into campground.

I'll walk into heab'n and take my seat,
And cast my crown at Jesus' feet.
   Lord, I want to cross over into campground,
   Lord, I want to cross over into campground,
   Lord, I want to cross over into campground.

Deep river, my home is over Jordan;
Deep river, Lord, I want to cross over into campground.
   Lord, I want to cross over into campground,
   Lord, I want to cross over into campground,
   Lord, I want to cross over into campground.

Deep calleth unto deep at the noise of thy waterspouts: thy waves and thy billows are gone over me.—Psalm 42:7

In this song the slave singers took a page out of the book of ancient Hebrew history. In a profound and symbolic way they identified with the Hebrews, who under the leadership of the young commander Joshua stood on the banks of the Jordan opposite the promised land and awaited the parting of the waters so that they might cross over.

They pictured themselves standing on the banks of the symbolic river that separated them from the land of hope and promise. They too, like the ancient Hebrews, awaited marching orders and a dramatic deliverance.

It is interesting to note just how many times the slaves refer to this "river" in their beautiful and dramatic songs. "Deep River"; "O Wasn't That a Wide River"; "Roll, Jordan, Roll"; "Stand Still, Jordan"; and "You Must Have That True Religion, Or You Can't Cross There" are some of the many slave songs that helped establish this motif.

For the slaves the deep river was symbolic of the great divide. It separated their world of slavery from the world of freedom to which they knew they had been called. It separated their world of hope from the world of bitter frustration. Using the picture of the deep river was the slaves' way of expressing their feelings of complete alienation from the world of their brothers. Though the river was deep and threatening, they took their stance on its bank hopefully, expectantly, and sometimes triumphantly, as they viewed the land of promise. They knew that they were captives in an alien land. They knew in their hearts that they were born to be free. They expressed no doubt that their land, their home, and their true destiny lay beyond this "river" of their immediate experiences.

"Deep river, my home is over Jordan," A slave always knew in his heart that as a slave, the forced servant of his brothers, he was not and could not be at home. His true home, his

24

true selfhood, his personhood lay beyond the river of torture, trials, tears, and forced separation. He took his stance on the riverbank and cried out in protest: "This state is not my home." One can note in this song as well as in many others that in spite of the dehumanizing effect of slavery upon the soul of the slave he never retreated from the banks of hope and assurance that God's Promised Land was for him as well as for God's other children. He continued to sing out even in the midst of his frustrated hopes and thwarted ambitions: "My home is over Jordan."

In the following expression we observe an example of rare genius and creativity. "Deep River, I want to cross over into campground." A slave could not expose to his master his deep determination to throw off the yoke of slavery. So he artfully disguised his ambition by making it appear that he was only waiting for the chariot to swing low and carry him off to heaven. Of course this was only part of the truth. All slaves wanted to be carried away from the world of slavery to the campground of freedom, but freedom first of all here on earth among their brothers, and then freedom as a heavenly reward. When the masters heard them singing of the campground, they thought, as the slaves intended: Oh, how beautiful are their songs and, oh, how hopefully they speak of heaven!

It is also arresting to note the skill with which the slaves sought to bolster the morale of their comrades through songs. In their warm and emotionally charged worship services they would say to one another: "O children, O don't you want to go . . . to that Promised Land where all is peace?" There surely must have been, in response to this invitation, a rapturous "amen!" The slaves knew they were being reminded that their home lay beyond the bitter experiences of slavery and they must never lose heart. They must untiringly press forward and await their deliverance.

Although the spirit of protest against the conditions of slavery is very pronounced in this song, so also is an expression of a deep, profound though simple and childlike faith in God. The words express faith in a God who has everything to do with human affairs: The God who parted the river Jordan for his Hebrew children will surely cause the waters of a figurative Jordan to roll back for his slave children to admit them to that freedom they long to see. The slaves believed that they were moving as directly under the leadership of Almighty God as did the ancient Hebrews, with whom they so often identified themselves.

In this song is also an indication that the slaves, while looking for a home of earthly freedom, felt themselves also to be poor pilgrims of earth looking for a heavenly home. They sang about two rivers. Thus they viewed hopefully two promised lands. Their faith led them to believe that when they had finished their earthly pilgrimage they would "gather at Jesus' feet." They would await a dramatic parting of the waters, which would open the way to their land of freedom.

Finally, the beauty and glory of this song lies in the fact that it speaks so eloquently to our day and time. For deep, wide, and rolling are the rivers that flow among us. We are perhaps more conscious of the rivers that divide us than ever before. But we must not forget that rivers need not and do not always divide; they often connect. They present challenges to us to build bridges. Beyond them often lie great and wonderful promised lands. Our home—the true home for all God's children—lies beyond all these deep, man-made rivers that divide.

26

Keep Me f'om Sinkin' Down

Oh, Lord, oh, my Lord! Oh, my good Lord!
  Keep me f'om sinkin' down.
Oh, Lord, oh, my Lord! Oh, my good Lord!
  Keep me f'om sinkin' down.

I tell what I mean to do,
  Keep me f'om sinkin' down:
I mean to go to heab'n too,
  Keep me f'om sinkin' down.

I look up yonder an' what do I see?
  Keep me f'om sinkin' down.
I see de angels beckonin' me,
  Keep me f'om sinkin' down.

Deliver me out of the mire, and let me not sink: let me be delivered from them that hate me, and out of the deep waters. Let not the waterflood overflow me, neither let the deep swallow me up, and let not the pit shut her mouth upon me.—Psalm 69:114-15

The singers of this moving song spoke out in lamentable tones concerning the terrible fact that they had been encircled by trouble and affliction. They described themselves and their condition as people sinking into deep mire, who

27

try as they might, could find no rescue; whose every effort to extricate themselves only sent them deeper. They also described themselves as those who had come into deep waters, where floods were sweeping over their heads. It may have been the psalmist who inspired the slaves to use the image of persons caught in the mire and sinking down to describe themselves and their condition.

Frightening and bitter were the conditions of slavery, and only a strong will and the saving hand of God prevented the slave from sinking down mentally and emotionally. He sang as he struggled and pulled himself along through the mire: "Oh, Lord, oh, my Lord! Oh, my good Lord!/Keep me f'om sinkin' down!"

One can feel the pull and struggle in these words. There is the reaching up for more strength and the sure, helping hand of God. Hear the desperate cry of the slave for salvation, if not *from* the conditions of slavery, for God's sake, then in the midst of them. Keep me f'om sinkin' down.

We all have had to fight our way again and again through murky waters and swirling depths of human experiences. The slaves, to whom God gave such noble songs, have bequeathed to us a theme for our prayers as we pass through the deep and bitter experiences of life: Lord, keep me too from sinking down.

Perhaps the slaves prayed to be kept from sinking down into the certain mire of hate and bitterness. How easy and natural it would have been for them to bog down in the mire of hatred and bitterness of spirit. But, as their songs so well attest, somehow by God's grace they always managed to keep their heads above the waters. It is true that many of their songs did present their anguished cries from the deep, but in almost every case those cries from the deep cried

28

out unto the deep. The slaves looked to God for help and succor. This is the major difference, I believe, between the struggle of the slaves and the struggle of their children today. God seems to move too slowly for the children of the slaves, and they often struggle on without him. Not so, the slaves. Their songs, although originating in the dark and terrible valley, always ended more or less on the mountaintop with God. Their faith that God was leading in their fight steadied their steps and strengthened their wills.

The slaves were also constantly faced with the threat of sinking down in despair. Slavery was enough to drive anyone to despair. The pressure was enough to break even iron wills and spirits. For history has never known any form of human slavery worse than the slavery which the Negroes endured in America. For in it family life was completely destroyed. Children—even while babies—were sold away from mothers, and mothers from children. Fathers were often used only as animals. But the slave singers, instead of sinking down in utter despair, always pressed forward in a spirit of hope and determination. They would utter in the midnight hours: "Better days are a-coming, oh yes,/Better days are coming, oh yes." Surely they must have heard the quiet whisper of eternity as they passed through the waters of despair. "When thou passest through the waters, I will be with thee; and through the rivers, they shall not overflow thee." (Isaiah 43:2.) Many are the conditions of life that can lead to despair, for "into each life some rain *does* fall."

Sometimes life seems to be so terribly unmerciful; sometimes great avalanches of mud from unexpected floods come down upon us. In these seasons of potential despair the slave singers remind us again to pray: "Oh, Lord, oh, my good Lord, keep me f'om sinkin' down.

29

Finally, conditions were ripe for the slaves to sink down into the mire of sorrow and self-pity. Their plight was difficult and their burdens heavy indeed. They had to drink constantly from the bitter cup of sorrow and grief. They were a burdened people who knew trouble, and who sang about their troubles. Somehow they never sank beneath the waves of self-pity. They knew themselves to be a part of that great company of human sufferers who would be delivered by God. They expressed their belief in the following words:

My Lord delibered Daniel, Daniel, Daniel, Daniel,
My Lord delibered Daniel, and I know he will deliber me.
He delibered Daniel from de lion's den, Jonah from de belly ob de whale,
And de Hebrew children from de fiery furnace, and why not ebery man?

Their agony and suffering were great. But they were not unique in their suffering, and so they knew that they must not give in to self-pity. As deliverance had come to others, so it would come to them, in God's own good time. Suffering is indeed such an individual and lonely thing that eventually one will likely lose his footing and sink beneath the waves of self-pity, unless he is upheld by the hand of Him who assures us at all times that "underneath are His everlasting arms."

"I wait for the Lord, my soul doth wait, and in his word do I hope. My soul waiteth for the Lord more than they that watch for the morning. I say, more than they that watch for the morning" (Psalm 130:5-6).

Sometimes I Feel Like a Motherless Chile

Sometimes I feel like a motherless chile,
   Sometimes I feel like a motherless chile,
Sometimes I feel like a motherless chile,
   A long ways from home, a long ways from home.
True believer, a long ways from home,
   A long ways from home.

Sometimes I feel like I'm almos' gone,
   Sometimes I feel like I'm almos' gone.
Sometimes I feel like I'm almos' gone,
   'Way up in the heab'nly lan', 'way up in the
   heab'nly lan'.
True believer, 'way up in the heab'nly lan',
   'Way up in the heab'nly lan'.

Sometimes I feel like a motherless chile,
   Sometimes I feel like a motherless chile,
Sometimes I feel like a motherless chile,
   A long ways from home.

*My days are swifter than a weaver's shuttle, and are spent
without hope. O remember that my life is wind: mine eye
shall no more see good.—Job 7:6-7*

*Why died I not from the womb? Why did I not give up
the ghost when I came out of the belly? . . .*

For now should I have lain still and been quiet, I should have slept; then had I been at rest. . . .

There the wicked cease from troubling; and there the weary be at rest.

There the prisoners rest together; they hear not the voice of the oppressor.

The small and the great are there; and the servant is free from his master.

Wherefore is light given to him that is in misery, and life unto the bitter in soul.—Job 3:11, 13, 17-20

This is another of the sorrowful and mournful cries coming up out of that dark night of slavery. It expresses the deep feelings of despair and loneliness and helplessness that often characterized the lives of the slaves. Here the slaves sang sadly of their abode in a man-contrived hell.

By means of this song the slaves often talked to each other of their mutual feelings and conditions. Through their songs they often consoled and succored one another, for they all felt like motherless children, and so they were. They all shared a deep sense of defenselessness and haunting insecurity.

Feeling like a motherless child to the slaves meant also having no one to love them and to appreciate them for what they were as persons or for the limitless possibilities of what they might become as children of men and children of God. They knew that they were looked upon as God's stepchildren, not deserving of the right to become; as having no capacity to become anything other than slaves. They felt that they were loved and appreciated only as beasts of burden and for what comforts they could bring to others. There surely can be no starvation like the starvation of the human soul when it is bereft of real love and sympathy, of understanding and respect.

As the slaves sang of their deep feeling, they were describing their sense of lostness. They knew themselves to be the uprooted, the dispossessed, the disinherited. They knew that they had no real place on which to stand, no real place to which they could return. For they were not only physically uprooted and a "long ways from home," as they so often sang, but they were spiritually uprooted and a long ways from any home. They knew themselves to be a long way from any true home of fellowship and brotherhood, and human acceptance. They knew that their true home was not the slave cabin. In that status they always felt like motherless children. They were a long way from their true home of freedom, dignity, and human worth. Thus they would often sing:

> Sometimes I'm tossed and driven,
> Sometimes I don't know where to roam,
> I heard of a city called heaven,
> And I started to make it my home.

Again as our singers sang of their feelings of motherlessness, they were trying to describe their condition as "living on the outside." They always felt that as slaves they were on the outside of the real and true life looking in. They knew themselves to be excluded from a meaningful and purposeful life. They described themselves as poor pilgrims of sorrow. Perhaps the loneliest loneliness of life is to be surrounded by others and yet be left out, just left alone. Perhaps the saddest sadness is that of being alone and on the outside in one's sadness. The most sorrowful of all sorrows is sorrow one must bear alone on the outside. No broken-heartedness can compare with brokenheartedness one must bear alone. Yes indeed, to be on the outside as were the slaves is to feel like a motherless child.

It is significant and certainly no accident that the slaves used this picture in describing their limited and circumscribed relationship to their environment. And what an unhappy picture it is! Psychologists tell us that terrible and devastating effects are suffered by a child who is brought up without a sense of belonging, without any motherly care, without some loving person to kiss away the tears and to love away the little hurts and bruises. The hurt, bruised, and crushed souls of the slaves reached out for the touch of tender hands and found none there. They felt only the emptiness and coldness that come to motherless children.

Let us remember that through their deeply moving, sorrowful songs the slave singers may have sought to touch the religious conscience of their oppressors. They appealed to them in the name and spirit of their own religion. What Christlike souls could be so deaf as not to hear and respond in love and sympathy to that mournful cry, "Sometimes I feel like a motherless chile, a long ways from home!"?

Then in order to further disguise their protest and, at the same time, to more surely express their homelessness the slaves would sing:

> Sometimes I feel like I'm almos' gone,
> 'Way up in de heab'nly lan', 'way up in de
> heab'nly lan'.

Who would suspect a song with such an ending to express a spirit of protest? The poor slaves were thought by their masters to be longing for the heavenly land. But ah, no! They did feel sometimes, it is true, like taking their hands off the plow. They did wish sometimes that they could fly away and be at rest. However, they also envisioned the day when they could look behind them in this life and view the old days of slavery and all of its bitterness and sorrow. For this they never ceased to long or to pray. Of course, when life's race had been run and its work well done, they knew that they would go to the heavenly land and there rejoin mother and loved ones and leave far behind forever the gnawing sense of feeling like a motherless child.

Oh, Fix Me

Oh, oh, fix me! Oh, oh, fix me, Jesus!
Oh, oh, fix me, Jesus!
Oh, oh, fix me!

Fix me, Jesus, fix me!
Fix me for my long white robe,
Fix me, Jesus, fix me!

Fix me, Jesus , fix me!
Fix me for my starry crown,
Fix me, Jesus, fix me!

Fix me, Jesus, fix me!
Fix me for my journey home,
Fix me, Jesus, fix me!

For I delight in the law of God, in my inmost self, but I see in my members another law at war with the law of my mind and making me captive to the law of sin which dwells in my members. Wretched man that I am! Who will deliver me from the body of death? Thanks be to God through Jesus Christ our Lord.—Romans 7:22-25 RSV

Purge me with hyssop, and I shall be clean; wash me, and I shall be whiter than snow. . . . Create in me a clean heart, O God; and renew a right spirit within me.—
Psalm 51:7, 10

William James, in his *Varieties of Religious Experiences,* observed: "However widely the various religions of the world may differ, there are two things they have in common, viz., a sense that there is something wrong about us as we naturally stand, and a sense that we are saved from this wrongness by making proper connection with the higher power." Our "black and unknown bards" felt this universal soul-infecting wrongness in their own hearts and expressed the ageless yearning to be put right in their own simple and penetrating words: "Oh, oh, fix me! Oh, oh, fix me, Jesus! Oh, oh, fix me!"

It seems to me that in this simple petition, made by an untutored people, we meet the same desperate need expressed in the classic words of Paul: "Wretched man that I am, who will deliver me?" There is a great disparity between that which I know I ought to do and that which I really do.

Edward Sanford Martin, in his poem "My Name Is Legion," expressed it like this:

Within my earthly temple there's a crowd;
There's one of us that's humble, one that's proud,
There's one that's broken-hearted for his sins,
There's one that unrepentant sits and grins;
There's one that loves his neighbor as himself,
And one that cares for naught but fame and pelf.
From much corroding care I should be free
If I could once determine which is me.

The slaves continued to express the need to be fixed and fixed rightly as they sang, "I can't pray until you fix me right, I can't sing until you fix me right, I can't preach until you fix me right." And finally, "I'll go anywhere if you fix me right. Fix me, Jesus, fix me right."

We all know something of this need, this seeming "sickness unto death." We know something of the impotence of the will and desire as we naturally stand. We know something of the deep abiding need to be fixed, to be put right, to be healed of our brokenness. "Prone to wonder, Lord, I feel it, / Prone to leave the God I love."

The singers remind us not only of man's urgent need to be fixed, but also of man's utter inability to fix himself. This song implies that man's sickness of soul reaches to the very depths of his being. Not only is he unable to heal himself, but also, in and of himself he cannot even know his exceeding sinfulness. The psychologists are constantly reminding us just how prone we are to bias toward ourselves. We cannot objectively analyze ourselves. We can only see the corrupt self with our corrupt eyes. In this simple but all searching prayer "Oh, fix me," is expressed the deep yearning of the heart to know even something of the terrible corruption of the inner man. During the great revival days of my boyhood, my foreparents used to pray, in line with the praying of their slave parents, that "their eyes would be turned into the depth of their own hearts." Isn't this an expression of the first great need of man, eyes with which to see his own heart, the ability to begin to measure his miserableness before God? We all need to understand what it really means to pray for God's saving grace.

I once saw an advertisement of a small-town blacksmith shop which read: WE WELD EVERYTHING BUT A BROKEN HEART. This struck me as being significant. Time has revealed to me that in his unmended broken heart is indeed where man's greatest need lies. Man's heart is broken by sin and guilt and waywardness, and isolation from God and

39

man. Here is where man needs a great physician, one who can weld a broken heart. The testimony of the saints is that the God of Jesus Christ is a specialist in welding and fixing broken hearts, broken lives, discarded lives, broken homes, and broken relationships. "O black and unknown bards," who knew so much about broken hearts, who felt in your own sensitive souls such a heavy burden of guilt, thank you for reminding us that only God can fix a broken heart.

The apostle Paul, immediately after his cry of despair, "O wretched man that I am!" said, "I thank God through Jesus Christ our Lord. . . . There is therefore now no condemnation to them which are in Christ Jesus."

Brother Lawrence, that blessed saint who sought to teach us the meaning of practicing the presence of God, often prayed to his Lord thus: "I shall never do otherwise, if Thou leavest me to myself; it is Thou who must hinder my fall and mend what is amiss."

The writer of the fifty-first psalm, laboring under a crushing sense of sin, prayed that God would wash him and cleanse him of his great sins; but then he continued his prayer as if to say it is not enough, O God, to just cleanse me of past sins and rid me of my present burdens. But if I am to be fixed and fixed indeed, I must be cured and healed of my disposition to sin. And then he prayed "Make me a new heart, O God, and renew a right spirit within me." The psalmist knew that only to wash the old heart would leave it vulnerable to the onslaught of additional sins.

St. Augustine, in reflecting on the great power of his Lord to heal and to keep well, said in his *Confessions*, "Since Thou gavest me continency, I have observed it; but I retain the memory of evil habits, and their images come up oft before me. Thou has disentangled me from the delight of the ear and from the lust of the eyes. Into many snares of the senses my mind wanders miserably, but Thou pluckest me out mercifully. By pride, vain glory and love of praise I am tempted, but I seek Thy mercy till what is lacking in me by Thee be renewed and perfected."

My eldest daughter, at the age of two and one half or three years, used to say to us, when she was chastised for some little wrong she had done, "It was not I who did that; that was another little girl in me." The apostle Paul used a similar expression, "It is no longer I that live, but Christ in me." He was no longer the wretched man; his was no longer the divided heart; his was no longer the split will. He knew himself to have been crucified with Christ. The love of Christ now controlled him.

Surely man as he naturally stands needs to be fixed; anyone who knows anything about his own heart knows that he cannot fix himself, for the whole man is sick to the very depth of the soul. But thanks be to God, his unspeakable mercy and his immeasurable grace, always do abound, even for the chief of sinners.

Finally, the slave singers, knowing themselves to be ever following the leadership of God, always felt that they were facing some dramatic and eventful moment. Maybe the moment was very near when God would deliver them from bondage; maybe some were approaching the moment when their long white robes of victory would be delivered to them; maybe the divine hand was almost ready to place upon their tired and weary heads their starry crowns, or maybe they were ready to embark upon their final journey home. For

41

whatever event God would call them they wanted to be prepared, and so they prayed and sang, with hearts filled with glorious expectancy:

> Oh, oh, fix me!
> Fix me, Jesus, fix me!
> Fix me for my long white robe.
> Fix me for my starry crown.
> Fix me for my journey home.
> Fix me, Jesus, fix me!

Walk Togedder, Children

Oh, walk togedder, children, don't you get weary,
   Walk togedder, children, don't you get weary,
Oh, walk together, children, don't you get weary,
   Dere's a great camp meetin' in de Promised Land.
Gwine to mourn, and nebber tire;
   Mourn an' nebber tire; mourn an' nebber tire;
Dere's a great camp meetin' in de Promised Land.

Oh, get you ready, children, don't you get weary;
   Get you ready, children, don't you get weary;
We'll enter dere, oh children, don't you get weary,
   Dere's a great camp meetin' in de Promised Land.
Goin' to pray and nebber tire;
   Pray and nebber tire; pray and nebber tire,
Dere's a great camp meetin' in de Promised Land.

*If two of you shall agree on earth as touching anything that
they shall ask, it shall be done for them of my Father which
is in heaven. For where two or three are gathered together
in my name, there am I in the midst of them.—*
Matthew 19:19-20

*Can two walk together, except they be agreed?—*Amos 3:3

*After that he appeared in another form unto two of them,
as they walked and went into the country.—*Mark 16:12

43

. . . When his candle shined upon my head, and when by his light I walked through darkness.—Job 29:3

The untutored slave singers always interpreted their lives as a sure pilgrimage. This picture of the lonely pilgrim appears again and again in their beautiful and arresting songs. The ugly and bitter realities of slavery drained their everyday life of its joy, happiness, and true meaning. They knew that if they were to have a life of real meaning and purpose, it lay in the distance before them. They were sure that their whole life was only another Exodus under God. Thus they always felt that their sojourn in slavery was but a passage through a dark and unsympathetic night. Some day, they were convinced, they would emerge beyond that dark and terrifying night in sight of the beautiful Promised Land. So they often sang as they marched, "I'm so glad troubles don't last always."

But as surely as slavery was passing away, they realized, this earthly life, for them and for all mankind, was also fleeting. So in another true sense they saw all human life as an Exodus. In many of their beautiful and soul-stirring songs there appears the uncanny, artistic interweaving of the fleeting quality of life, the conviction that the institution of human slavery had in itself the seeds of death, and the happy assurance that they were marching toward that glorious day in the beautiful city of God. One cannot really understand the Negro spirituals in their true meaning unless he keeps in mind the fact that however deeply religious they were meant to be, they were truly protest songs, pep songs, morale builders, songs alive with the slaves' faith and determination to outlive slavery.

44

The undaunted souls of slavery trudging through their terrible valley of sorrow often reminded each other that they were indeed fellow travelers, strangers and pilgrims in the world, ever looking for a better home. They would sing to one another on this order: "Brothers, we must walk together. Our burdens are too heavy to carry alone, the journey to freedom is too long and too perilous; we will surely faint, and our wills and spirits will surely be broken if we do not walk together." They could not afford the luxury of division; their common lot was too grave. It is in this spirit that we must hear the solemn admonition of the slaves: Walk to-gedder, children.

The slaves never doubted that there would be a great camp meeting in the Promised Land. They knew in their hearts that God had promised them a land of freedom and fulfillment as surely as he had promised the Hebrews of old, with whom they so often identified themselves. The assurance that a great day of deliverance was coming was so real for burdened singers that they could shout even in chains and from their shanties: "Get you ready, children, don't you get weary. Dere's a great camp meeting in de Promised Land." They did not always sing of a far-off promised land for the spirit after death, though this was never out of their minds, but often of a promised land here and now, where their children could shout in freedom and never tire. Their hopes and their prayers must find complete fulfillment in this great land of ours, this "land of the free and the home of the brave." For the Promised Land of the slaves is inextricably bound up with the great promise extended to all Americans.

This simple picture of walking together may well have come to the minds and hearts of the slaves at a time when

45

some of their members were seeking escape from bondage by way of the underground railroad. Some may already have been hiding awaiting the signal to move, and these words were sung for the benefit of the timid and weary: "Remember, always walk togedder, children." They knew that in walking together they would have the comfort, strength, and security of one another. How relevant are these wonderful words for our day. We too are walking through the dark ways and byways of life, haunted and molested by racial and class bigotry, envy, hatred, and greed; in this day of stark and threatening divisions in our land—poverty and affluence, black and white extremists, ghettoes and suburbia, hawks and doves—we must learn to walk together in mutual help and trust. The simple words of the slaves ring loud and clear today to all that have ears to hear and hearts to understand: Walk togedder, children, or, we may well add, we may not walk at all.

There is a promised land for all, and a great camp meeting for all, but it seems quite clear that God has ordained that none shall reach this promised land alone. If we are to arrive in this land of peace, security, and freedom, we must surely go there hand in hand.

My Lord's A-Writin' All de Time

Come down, come down, my Lord, come down,
   My Lord's a-writin' all de time;
And take me up to wear the crown,
   My Lord's a-writin' all de time.

King Jesus rides in de middle of de air,
   My Lord's a-writin' all de time.
He's callin' sinners from ev'rywhere,
   My Lord's a-writin' all de time.

Oh, he sees all you do, he hears all you say,
   My Lord's a-writin' all de time.
Oh, he sees all you do, he hears all you say,
   My Lord's a-writin' all de time.

Out of the abundance of the heart the mouth speaketh. A good man out of the good treasure of the heart bringeth forth good things; and an evil man out of the evil treasure bringeth forth evil things. But I say unto you that every idle word that men shall speak they shall give an account thereof in the day of judgment.—Matthew 12:34b-36

There is a profound, frightening, and shattering truth in this simple, almost naïve picture of God that the black poet-singers throw on the canvas of their imagination: The great

47

God of the universe, with his all-seeing eye, sitting upon his great white throne holding the open book on whose pages appears the life's record of every man, and meticulously jotting down all that everyone does and says. These simple people had no doubts about man's accountability to God for all that he should do or say. Herein lies the great stabbing truth of this song, man's accountability to God.

It seems to me that those untutored slave singers have much to say to us today about ourselves if we are not too busy and too proud to listen. For the startling and arresting expression "He sees all you do, and he hears all you say" deals more with ourselves than with God; for man indeed is ever writing all the time, whether he is conscious of it or not.

Our blessed Lord, mankind's greatest teacher, with his penetrating analysis of human life, reminded his hearers that not even one idle word that falls from men's lips can escape that ultimate accounting. For God knew what was in man and knew better than any psychologist that words flow from the fountains of the thoughts and thoughts flow from the heart. "Out of the heart come the issues of life"; "Out of the abundance of the heart the mouth speaketh"; "Make the tree good and the fruit good, or make the tree evil and the fruit evil."

This is one of the great lessons that we can gather from this simple song for today; man, every man, not God, is writing all the time. This is indeed one of the great spiritual insights which those unknown bards came to share. They knew in their own hearts that there was somewhere an eternal eye that sees all, even the very depths of men's hearts, and an eternal ear that hears all, even man's innermost thoughts, and an eternal hand that records all. This they said to themselves, but most especially to their masters. or they had no doubts that their oppressors would have to stand before God.

It is terrifying to be so dramatically reminded that our thoughts are actually deeds; deeds of the very heart. The issues of life come from the heart, but one's thoughts continually and finally determine the kind of heart out of which they come. The very character of the inner springs of life is being determined every moment. All of life, every bit of it, is therefore infinitely important. Time never simply passes; all moments have eternal significance.

It is true, however, not only that thoughts are deeds, but that words are deeds also. Words, whether idle or profound, tell what is going on behind the closed doors of men's hearts. They reveal one's deep interests, one's pressing concerns, one's cares and indifferences, loves and hates. Listen to one's conversation long enough and it will reveal his heart; it will tell you where his real treasures lie.

The awful judgment described by the slave singers in this dramatic language may well remind us that God has built into the very fabric of our souls a transcribing process, by which every thought, every word, and every deed is indelibly registered. The psalmist of old cried out, "O Lord, thou hast searched me, and known me. Thou knowest my downsitting and mine uprising, thou understandest my thought afar off. Thou . . . art acquainted with all my ways. For there is not a word in my tongue, but, lo, O Lord, thou knowest it altogether" (Psalm 139:1-4).

How searching and penetrating is this thought. But not only is it true that God's all-seeing eye reveals all about us, but also all the idle dreams we entertain, every idle word

49

we speak, and all we do is recorded on a most sensitive plate hidden within the deep recesses of our very being. These things eternally affect our lives, shape our character, and ultimately determine our destinies.

This truth was brought out in the television comedy "Our Miss Brooks." In one episode Principal Conklin and his faculty members were making elaborate preparations for a visit by the distinguished members of the school board. In preparation for this visit Principal Conklin, Miss Brooks, and other proposed speakers decided to record their speeches so they could simply go through the motions of speaking while the recorder delivered their messages to the school board. This would eliminate their excessive nervousness. But, alas, some culprit found the tape and cut it into a number of pieces, thus disjoining the speeches. Then he set about in haste to rejoin it. But in the process he had bits of Mr. Conklin's speech here and there (all out of order), and sandwiched between broken bits of Miss Brooks's and others' speeches. As a result, when the distinguished guests arrived and Mr. Conklin stood to deliver his speech, the tape played back a completely jumbled speech. What utter chaos filled the house! Is this not a true picture of man's life? The hidden recordings of our hate and envy, our grudges, prejudices, and jealousies are ever being played back into our conscious lives. These make up the sum total of the man. These make up our true personalities.

What a judgment! What I am I have chosen to be, in spite of God's earnest plea that I, by his help and grace, become something better. Maybe Mohammud was not too far from the truth when he pictured man in the last judgment standing before the judgment seat with his record hanging about his neck, written in his own hand. Would he not, however, have been even nearer the frightening and devastating truth had he pictured the record as written in our own handwriting and in our own hearts?

This picture suggested by the slave singers may well remind us not only that we stand completely naked before God, but also that we cannot completely hide ourselves from others. Somehow we are always communicating ourselves to others no matter how hard we may try to conceal ourselves. We are always sending out vibrations, vibrations from the true inner self that tell whether they come from centers of love or hate, peace or turbulence, hope or despair. Sooner or later men come to know our real selves. Even little children can very quickly discern whether we are real or false. Yes, my Lord's writing all the time. Kierkegaard says that things cannot be hidden ultimately but are always reflected in the mirror in which nothing can be concealed. Does anyone really believe that his most secret thoughts and desires are not manifest in the whole being or that the events within the darkness of his subconscious or in the isolation of his consciousness do not produce eternal repercussions?

A friend once said to me, "You know, God permits us to make our faces." She went on, "He gives us only the broad outlines and gives us the privilege of filling in." And what a privilege! And what a burden! This is truly what we are doing all the time. We are filling in and thus making our faces. The faces we see about us every day are faces drawn by men: Faces that shine with happiness and contentment; faces that wear the furrows of worry, fear, anxiety, dread, doubt, and despair; faces that are careworn; faces that bear the lines of crime and deceit and hypocrisy; faces that reflect trust, assurance, confidence, obedience, and worthy com-

mitment; faces that are straightforward ever pressing on-
ward, upward. Yes, they are all about us, this sea of faces
drawn by men. My Lord's writing all the time, and he sees
all we do and he hears all we say.

There is something marvelously beautiful about the word
pictures of our Lord and his unique power to communicate
himself to those about him. The woman with the issue of
blood felt his power and she was healed. Mary and Martha
were sure that if he had only been near their brother would
not have died. The frightened and panicking disciples on
the storm-tossed waters saw his awakening presence make
a mighty calm. Zaccheus looked on his glowing face and
it inspired new life and kindled a new spark in his soul. The
condemned and sinful woman beheld his eyes of hope and
understanding and went away forgiven. Yes, for good or for
woe we are always communicating ourselves to others. Try
as we may, we cannot hide our secret sins or our secret
beneficent deeds. They will surely find us out. This is the
judgment.

Those unknown bards reminded us in very descriptive
language that our Lord is writing all the time. Every day
we stand completely unclothed before his awful presence.
Every moment his all-seeing eyes search us to the very depths.
There are days and moments, of course, when judgment is
more dramatic, but every day we stand completely revealed.

Confronted as we are by this awful truth of life, that
our God sees all we do and hears all we say, and that he is
writing all the time, what must we do to be saved? We surely
know that what he has heard and seen taking place in our
lives has not been a holy sight. Therefore, our only hope is
to come before God in deep contrition and repentance and
humility and to pray with the psalmist, "Cleanse thou me

52

from secret faults. . . . Let the words of my mouth, and the meditation of my heart, be acceptable in thy sight, O Lord, my strength, and my redeemer. Search me, O God, and know my heart: try me, and know my thoughts: And see if there be any wicked way in me, and lead me in the way everlasting."

Oh Mary,
Don't You Weep,
Don't You Mourn

O Mary, don't you weep, don't you mourn,
   O Mary, don't you weep, don't you mourn.
Pharaoh's army got drownded.
   O Mary, don't you weep.

Sister, what do you want to stay here for?
   Dis old world is no place to live;
Pharaoh's army got drownded.
   O Mary, don't you weep.

Brother, what do you want to stay here for?
   Dis old world is no place to live;
Pharaoh's army got drownded.
   O Mary, don't you weep.

*The Jews then which were with her in the house, and com-
forted her, when they saw Mary, that she rose up hastily and
went out, followed her, saying, She goeth unto the grave to
weep there. Then when Mary was come where Jesus was,
and saw him, she fell down at his feet, saying unto him,
Lord, if thou hadst been here, my brother had not died.—*
John 11:31-32.

*The first day of the week cometh Mary Magdalene early,
when it was yet dark, unto the sepulchre, and seeth the stone*

taken away from the sepulchre. Then she runneth, and cometh to Simon Peter, and to the other disciple, whom Jesus loved, and saith unto them, They have taken away the Lord out of the sepulchre, and we know not where they have laid him. . . . Mary stood without at the sepulchre weeping: and as she wept, she stooped down, and looked into the sepulchre. . . . She turned herself back and saw Jesus.—John 20: 1-2, 11, 14

This song exhibits one of the most masterful pieces of deception and yet served one of the most noble ends. By recalling the precious name of Mary and subtly recalling two of the most dramatic moments of New Testament experience, the slaves appeared to be singing only of the great events of the past and of their great hope of heaven someday. This, of course, was most comforting to their masters, and thus served its purpose well. But far more important for the slaves, they were singing about their plight of slavery. In the name of the God of the New Testament they were protesting the evils of slavery and were comforting one another. This song was addressed primarily to themselves but secondarily to their masters. To their own they were offering hope, comfort, and assurance; to their masters they were predicting the fall of slavery. Together in their spirited meetings they would sing of God's great deliverance of the past and how this past, in the most meaningful way, came to bear upon their own present condition and their hope for the future.

This song is, like many other great spirituals, a sublime expression of the slaves' faith in God. Their God has to do with history and the causes of men. They could reason:

Just as God fought on the side of his people Israel and destroyed Pharaoh's army before them, so he will fight for our deliverance. Again they could reason that though their cause sometimes seemed dead like Lazarus of old, the one who called forth Lazarus from the grave could surely revive their cause. By taking the long, backward look at God's mighty working in history, the slaves were always able to take the long forward look with God.

To the timid and unadventurous souls among them, the slaves would sing: "Sister, what do you want to stay here for? This old world is no place to live. Pharaoh's army got drownded, Oh, Mary, don't you weep." Yes, they were saying: We must not allow ourselves to lie down before the conditions of slavery; these conditions are intolerable, this is no world in which to live. God is calling us to a fuller life and a more meaningful purpose. We must be ever prepared to march forward with him. We must not destroy ourselves or lay waste our energies by weeping and mourning; we must rise up and gird our loins for the journey toward the land of freedom, for we will accept no other world.

When one examines a great song such as this that came out of the abyss of slavery, he will very soon come to understand just why the slaves exhibited such patience and endurance, and even such apparent joy. To the slaves God was very real and near. All the forces of nature stood ready to do his will. They believed that no powers, be they ever so firmly entrenched, could ultimately frustrate or defeat God's purpose. They believed that God demanded that all his children be free. They believed with all their hearts that their cause—just simple freedom—was in God's eternal hands. They

57

believed that anyone or any system built across God's purpose would surely be destroyed. Thus they could sing with great enthusiasm:

> O Mary, don't you weep, don't you mourn.
> Pharaoh's army got drownded,
> O Mary, don't you weep.

Dere's No Hidin' Place Down Dere

Dere's no hidin' place down dere,
Dere's no hidin' place down dere.
Oh, I went to de rocks to hide my face,
De rocks cried out, "No hidin' place,"
Dere's no hidin' place down dere.

Poor sinner man, he stumbled and fell,
He tried to go to heab'n, but had to go to hell,
Dere's no hidin' place down dere.

*Whither shall I go from thy spirit? or whither shall I flee
from thy presence? If I ascend up into heaven, thou art
there: if I make my bed in hell, behold, thou art there.—*
Psalm 139:7-8.

*And the kings of the earth, and the great men, and the
rich men, and the chief captains, and the mighty men, and
every bondman, and every free man, hid themselves in the
dens and in the rocks of the mountains; and said to the
mountains and rocks, Fall on us and hide us from the face
of him that sitteth on the throne, and from the wrath of the
Lamb; For the great day of his wrath is come; and who shall
be able to stand?—Revelation 6:15-17.*

This song like so many of the great spirituals, speaks with
a shattering ring of eternity about it. It tells us what we

already know of ourselves; that we cannot hide and yet how often we try to hide. The hearts and minds of the slave singers were saturated with vivid and poetic pictures of the omnipresence of God. As they sang this song, they surely must have had in mind the frightening word picture of the psalmist: "Whither shall I go from thy spirit?" Or they may have recalled the frightening picture in the book of Revelation where men are running and crying unto the rocks and the mountains to fall on them and hide them from the face of an angry God. They sang, "I went to the rocks to hide my face, the rocks cried out, 'no hiding place.'" Even nature's most secret and secure places offered no hiding place.

How many times and in how many ways have we all tried to escape the realities of life; God, ourselves, our secret sins, our guilt, our fears, and our anxieties. And yet wherever we go, we hear the still, small, and disturbing voice, "there's no hiding place down dere." We know that to live is to be sought and found. Wherever men take life seriously, they will recognize that they are eternally indebted to these unknown singers for the simple and yet pungent way by which mankind is reminded of his unique spiritual predicament. From life's most serious moments no man can ultimately hide.

Often, in this busy day, we try to hide in the crowd. We seek to get lost. But even here we are sought out and found. God has created every one of us in a unique way. He has made us so that no one person has fingerprints like another. No wonder the psalmist said: "My substance was not hid from thee, when I was made in secret, and curiously wrought in the lowest parts of the earth. Thine eyes did see my substance; . . . and in thy book all my members were written"

60

(Psalm 139:15-16). No, we cannot lose ourselves in the crowd. Talk with a mother of many children about her dear ones and she will describe every one in different terms. They are indeed all different.

This disturbing song can well remind us that there are times when men seek to hide themselves behind the smoke screen of their own hallowed tradition. They often resort to misreading the facts of history, ignoring the hard-won truths of scientists, and even the impossible straining of the interpretations of the blessed Scriptures. But before the searching light of truth as God has revealed it, there is no hiding place even down there.

Then why do we try to hide from God? Do we not try to hide because we know deep down that our lives are often empty and hollow? We know that we cannot stand before the all-revealing truth of God, so we try to hide. Like Adam, we know that we are naked and that our lives are shabby, and we are ashamed, and we seek to hide. A few years ago, a man involved in one of the most noted crimes of our time confessed that even though he was able to elude the law for quite a while, he was always scared to death. When someone would call or a stranger would appear, he was frightened. We too try to hide because we know that our lives are often deeply involved in pretense and hypocrisy. We are afraid that we too will be found out because the still, small voice continues to whisper in our hearts that there's no lasting hiding place down there.

Again the slaves knew that men try to hide from God because of their restless sense of sin. We know that again and again we have done those things we ought not to have done, and we have left undone those things we ought to have done. Our secret sins are ever before us. We are not

61

quite ready to accept our heavenly Father's comforting and healing forgiveness. We are not quite prepared to make a clean break with our sins. We love them, we enjoy them, even though they wound us. We love them, and so we try to hide from God in order that we may enjoy our sins for at least a brief season. We are going to break with sin someday—maybe soon—but not now. So in our quiet moments, in the midst of our sins, the disturbing words come to us: There is really no hiding place down there, not even in the enjoyment of these little sins. My foreparents used to sing another very striking spiritual akin to this one: "The secret's in your heart, you can't hide; the secret's in your heart, you can't hide; he sent me to tell you, you can't hide."

But thanks be to God the slave singers did not leave us to despair in singing "I went to the rocks to hide my face,/ The rocks cried out 'no hiding place.' " Because they could point us to another Rock in which we may find rest and security. Let us listen to them as they sing, with great assurance, that even though the rocks in the mountains crumble and decay, they have a home in that eternal Rock.

> I got a home in-a dat Rock, don't you see?
> I got a home in-a dat Rock, don't you see?
> Between de earth an' sky,
> Thought I heard my Saviour cry,
> You got a home in-a dat Rock, don't you see?

It is only in utter commitment to God and a complete surrendering of our wills to his will that we find life's true hiding place.

My Lord, What a Mornin'

My Lord, what a mornin', my Lord, what a mornin',
   My Lord, what a mornin', when de stars begin to fall.
My Lord, what a mornin', my Lord, what a mornin',
   My Lord, what a mornin', when de stars begin to fall.

You'll hear de trumpet sound, to wake de nations underground,
Lookin' to my God's right hand, when de stars begin to fall.

You'll hear de sinner moan, to wake de nations underground,
Lookin' to my God's right hand, when the stars begin to fall.

You'll hear de Christians shout, to wake de nations underground,
Lookin' to my God's right hand, when de stars begin to fall.

And I beheld when he had opened the sixth seal, and, lo, there was a great earthquake; and the sun became black as sackcloth of hair, and the moon became as blood; and the stars of heaven fell unto the earth, even as a fig tree casteth her untimely figs, when she is shaken of a mighty wind. And the heavens departed as a scroll when it is rolled together; and every mountain and island were moved out of their places.—Revelation 6:12-14

The New Testament writers often wrote in very picturesque language concerning the instability of all earthly things. They believed that they were living in two worlds, the passing and the coming. They believed that everything that seemed to be fixed and permanent in the old, evil world would surely pass away. They described this dramatic passing of the old in terms of the darkening of the sun; the moon going down in blood; the fixed stars falling from heaven; or the mountains, the islands, and the seas fleeing away.

The Negro slaves were gripped by this graphic and picturesque language of the New Testament, for like the New Testament writers they also lived in an intolerable day and under almost unbearable conditions. They too hoped for the swift and sudden passing of the established order of slavery with its bitter experiences. They too felt that they were living in two worlds; one, the present evil world of slavery, which was surely passing; and the other a world of freedom, which was rapidly approaching.

Thus the slaves, yearning for freedom and yet finding their hopes thwarted again and again, came to adopt this New Testament outlook on life and, with rare poetic genius, gave to the world this true and devastating song.

In this plaintive song they remind all human travelers that even the most fixed and secure stars of the heavens will someday surely fall. Life has taught most of us just how true this song is. For we have all felt the shaking of the old, once-secure foundations of life. We have all seen that which we held to be most permanent cut loose by the sharp edge of the unexpected and washed out to sea. We all know something of the blasting of life's fondest dreams; the loss of life's noblest ideals; the baffling of our surest hopes; and the thwarting of our most attractive ambitions. We have all awakened, or will surely awake, to face some empty and terrifying morning when the stars begin to fall.

The unknown bards surveyed the deeply entrenched social positions of their masters, and yet, by faith, they knew and could sing about the fact that change was already in the air. They knew in their hearts that the very foundations of this order would crumble. Let us always keep in mind that when slaves sang of that fateful morning when the stars would surely fall, they were speaking of the fall of slavery. They knew that if there was a God of justice and mercy working in human affairs, surely he would shorten the evil days which had brought such terrible assaults upon their souls. We all thank God today that the stars of that evil sky did fall.

This sorrowful and yet truthful song also suggests the impermanence of all material things. In our day, when there is the hungering and thirsting for more and more material things, we would do well to meditate upon these precious and soul-searching words, and be reminded that there is really no lasting security in anything material. He who puts his trust in material things will surely awaken to face that awful morning when the stars begin to fall.

We dare not forget those devastating words that our blessed Lord uttered to his disciples as they showed him the beautiful and seemingly eternal stones of the temple: "Verily I say unto you, there shall not be left here one stone upon another, that shall not be thrown down" (Matthew 24: 2b). Sometime ago I was impressed by an article entitled, "All That My Cold, Dead Hands Can Hold." Is it not true indeed that man's lasting security, if it is to be found at all, must be found in those things which will be left in his hands when they are cold and dead?

65

Paul has a sure word of encouragement for all of us who are aware of the transitoriness of all that we see. In companionship with the living Christ, Paul laid hold upon those values of life that do not pass away but grow more secure with every passing day. "No wonder we do not lose heart! Though our outward humanity is in decay, yet day by day we are inwardly renewed. . . . Meanwhile our eyes are fixed, not on the things that are seen, but on the things that are unseen: for what is seen passes away; what is unseen is eternal." (II Corinthians 4:16-20 NEB.)

Somebody's Knockin' at Your Door

Somebody's knockin' at your door, somebody's knockin' at
    your door;
O sinner, why don't you answer? Somebody's knockin' at
    your door.
  Knocks like Jesus, somebody's knockin' at your door;
  Knocks like Jesus, somebody's knockin' at your door.
O sinner, why don't you answer? Somebody's knockin' at
    your door.

You better let him in, somebody's knockin' at your door;
O sinner, why don't you answer? Somebody's knockin' at
    your door.
  Knocks like Jesus, somebody's knockin' at your door;
  Knocks like Jesus, somebody's knockin' at your door.
O sinner, why don't you answer? Somebody's knockin' at
    your door.

*Behold, I stand at the door and knock; if any man hear my
voice, and open the door, I will come in to him, and will
sup with him, and he with me.*—Revelation 3:20

This has always been for me one of the most arresting
of all the wonderful Negro spirituals. This song like many
of the great spirituals makes its appeal directly to the heart
of the hearer. Perhaps there is none that more definitely

67

and more persuasively asks for the human heart than this one. This particular spiritual is a rarity in that it does not have any undertones of protest. This is a deeply religious song.

I remember quite clearly, as a very small boy, hearing this song for the first time, as it was sung by my illiterate but devout grandmother. I was struck first, I believe, by its somber tone, and then by its piercing, simple, and searching words, 'Somebody's knockin' at your door." It seemed that the song was addressed to me and to me alone, although I doubt that my grandmother was even conscious of my listening to her singing, for she was going about the chores of the house. Ah, but what a personal appeal this special song had for me on that special day. It said to my little childish heart something that somehow I already knew: There was somebody knocking at my heart's door. I did not know who was knocking, but I was aware of the fact that he was no intruder, but one who somehow had a right to knock, and who had come to claim that which was his own. Power to evoke this response in the human breast is what gives to many of the Negro spirituals their universal appeal.

A young woman, visiting our church services for the first time a few years ago, was with us on the day I spoke on this simple theme. She later said that she had been followed and haunted all the following week by those simple words, "Somebody's knockin' at your door." And who is it who cannot say in response to these words, "Surely someone has been knocking at my door too."

This spiritual continues, "It knocks like Jesus." Jesus' knock is always a strange and disturbing one, and yet it is a familiar and friendly knock. We need to understand that he who is ever knocking is coming to bring us only that

68

which is best for us, and for which our hearts have really been yearning. To use his own blessed words, "I will come in to him, and will sup with him, and he with me." He comes that we may break our fast and begin to feast indeed. The slave singers knew what it meant to open to him and to feast with him, for it was the opening of the door and the coming in of Jesus that so often restored their weary souls.

When he knocks, we are often not quite ready for so divine a guest. We know that his coming will make us uncomfortable with many of our familiar guests and old friends. For our new guest, with his shattering knock, is friendly, and yet selective and exclusive. If he comes in, his very presence will demand the withdrawal, even the expulsion, of many of our familiar friends and guests.

The one who always stands at the door of our hearts knocking is none other than the blessed one who invited himself to the home of Zacchaeus. Somehow Jesus' spirit entered the very heart of Zacchaeus, and Jesus' entrance through that sad heart's door changed all things for this lonely man. The old guests of greed, lust, dishonesty, and covetousness, which had lingered so long with Zacchaeus draining and choking the fountains of love and sympathy, were summarily dismissed, and the wellsprings of joy and peace were opened for the first time in his life. He now knew that his old life, before Jesus came to visit him, was hardly life at all.

Surely the one who is knocking at your door and mine is none other than the blessed Savior.

The slave singers continued their warning, "you better let him in, somebody's knockin' at your door." Who has not heard this warning deep down in his heart of hearts? We who keep Jesus waiting outside the closed door of

69

our hearts do so at the peril of our very lives. His presence at the door of our hearts is not to be accepted or rejected lightly. for he has all to do with our destiny both in this world and in the world to come. "Today if ye will hear his voice, harden not your hearts." (Hebrews 3:7-8a.)

Those slave singers believed that there was something tragic indeed about turning a deaf ear to our Lord's knock. The longer we keep him waiting outside, the less sensitive to his rap we become. The rap is loud, clear, and unmuffled at first; but the longer we defer the opening of the door, the fainter the sound appears. Is not this the real death of the soul? To grow so insensitive to the precious knock and pleading of our Lord so as not to be able to hear any longer? For the Christ of God, the giver of life abundant and life eternal, to stand outside the door of a poor dying soul knocking and not being heard is for that soul to die the death of deaths. How truly they sang, "You better let him in, somebody's knockin' at your door."

From the first time I heard my grandmother intone these words until now I have not been able to get completely away from them. There are times, of course, when they sound more dramatic and more appealing than others; but, nevertheless, they are always there. Their refusal to go away reveals the wonder, patience, and mercy of our Christ. Even after years of partial surrender and half-hearted commitments on our part he continues to knock at the doors of all those uncommitted rooms of our lives. He asks for the very last key to even the smallest room of our hearts. He would have open access to all the rooms and little private places in our lives. He wants to bless us and completely possess us, for it is only in his complete possession that we really have peace. "Why don't you answer?" the singers con-

70

tinued. The voice comes, as our Christ asks of us each morning a sure and more definite commitment, a deeper concentration, and a higher devotion. Sometimes in his amazing mercy he comes in the stillness of the night when we are alone with our hearts. He knocks oh so gently in that quietness, and we can barely hear him. "Why don't you answer" and answer completely?

We shall be forever indebted to the slave singers, who presented the invitation of the living Christ in such beautiful and dramatic language, and who warned us in such stern language of the perils of refusing to open our hearts' doors.

I've Been 'Buked and I've Been Scorned

I've been 'buked and I've been scorned,
I've been 'buked and I've been scorned,
I've been talked about, sho' as you're born.

Dere is trouble all over dis world,
Dere is trouble all over dis world,
Children, dere is trouble all over dis world.

I ain't gwine to lay my 'ligion down,
I ain't gwine to lay my 'ligion down,
Children, I ain't gwine to lay my 'ligion down.

Thou makest us a reproach to our neighbours, a scorn and a derision to them that are round about us. Thou makest us a byword among the heathen, a shaking of the head among the people. My confusion is continually before me, and the shame of my face hath covered me, for the voice of him that reproacheth and blasphemeth; by reason of the enemy and avenger.—Psalm 44:13-16

For this thing I besought the Lord thrice, that it might depart from me. And he said unto me, My grace is sufficient for thee; for my strength is made perfect in weakness.—
II Corinthians 12:8-9a

Blessed are ye, when men shall revile you, and persecute you, and shall say all manner of evil against you falsely, for

73

my sake. Rejoice and be exceeding glad: for great is your reward in heaven.—Matthew 5:11-12a

Finally, my brethren, be strong in the Lord, and in the power of his might. Put on the whole armour of God, that ye may be able to stand against the wiles of the devil. For we wrestle not against flesh and blood, but against principalities, against powers, against the rulers of the darkness of this world, against spiritual wickedness in high places.—Ephesians 6:10-12

Slave singers used their songs in a unique way to describe and dramatize the terrible and devastating effect which slavery had upon them. This is a song whose very words and tones speak of the awful plight of the slaves. It tells of their sorrow, their horror, their resentment, and their protest. One needs to hear this song as the slaves sang it in order to really begin to understand how strongly they felt abut their treatment. For them slavery was vicious and abominable, and truly signified man's inhumanity to man. They sang out in utter disbelief that man could be so inhuman to man as to "buke" him and scorn him and talk about him every day and in every way.

Let us allow the slaves to tell their own story concerning that long, bitter, and black night. "I've been 'buked," they sang. It would seem at first that the singers were saying that they had been rebuked. I feel that instead of meaning that they had been rebuked or restrained, they were saying that they had been abused and misused—treated not as persons but as things. They were used for the gain of others. They protested the fact that they were being exploited and that their very lives were treated as something for

74

you reap a habit; Sow a habit, and you reap a character; Sow a character, and you reap a destiny."

The slaves were aware not only that each individual life is a field in which everyone is always sowing, but also that we are always sowing in a wider context, because each individual life is a part of the whole. For a truth, no one really sows to himself, and no one finally reaps unto himself. This is a terrible and frightening burden that all humans must bear. The expression "You goin' to reap just what you sow" could well be expanded to say, "You goin' to reap just what *he* sows, and he's goin' to reap just what you sow." I remember how my father and his neighbor used to plant their corn close together. One would plant white corn, while the other might plant yellow. The rows in each field that lay close to the other field would always bear varied coloring. You see, the pollen had blown from one field to the other, and each farmer not only reaped what he had sown, but also what the other had sown. How much like life this is: Our harvests are often inextricably tied with the harvests of others.

We all know something of the terrible and seemingly insoluble race problem in America. Is it not true that we are reaping this terrible harvest from what was sown in slavery, both white and black; this harvest of bitterness, resentfulness, separateness, and brokenness? The protest marches of today, the cries of injustice, even the terrible and frightening monsters of "Black Militancy" and the riots are all part of this awful reaping of what has been sown. God's eternal voice is heard in the midst of the charges and counter-charges. His voice of justice cries out in the midst of our streets and from the depths of the ghettoes, "I am not to be mocked. You've got to reap just what you sow." You must reap also just what the other man has sown.

79

In this song the slave singers sound a most solemn note of warning: Let him who would follow the path of evil beware of the certainty of reaping. We hear daily the expressions "Crime does not pay!"; "No one can beat the game!"; "You can't do wrong and get by!" The slaves believed from the depths of their hearts that slavery was wrong, and had within it the seeds of its own destruction. Did not these truths cry out to them from the Bible?

Adam sowed pride and self-will and reaped a cruel and stubborn sweat-drenched harvest beyond the gates of Eden. Cain sowed jealousy and murder and reaped a gnawing harvest and the haunting and ceaseless cry from eternity: "Where is thy brother?" David sowed lust and murder and reaped a bitter harvest of incest and fratricide.

The slave singers, however, not only sound a solemn note of warning in this song, but also strike a joyful note of hope. The faithful and true-hearted soul whose harvest is often long delayed need not grow weary in well-doing, for he can be certain that in due season he will reap. This faith and assurance enabled these burdened slaves to press on and to say: "Keep a-inching along." Such faith in the certainty of the operation of God's law of sowing and reaping kept alive the flame—the hope for freedom—in the bosom of the slaves, when their hope seemed to be entirely futile. Though the night of slavery was so dark and long and the day of freedom so hesitant in coming, the slaves could endure, for they believed that they were sowing under the guidance of God. Someday they would reap a blessed harvest.

My friend Dr. Ira B. Loud shared with me the following little verse, whose author is unknown. This verse expresses a profound truth. The faith of these weary-hearted slaves is revealed in these words:

80

He who does God's work will draw God's pay,
However long may seem the day;
However weary is the way,
Though captains and kings thunder nay!
God does not pay as others pay
In silver, gold, and raiments gay;
But God's high wisdom knows the way,
And this is sure—let come what may,
If you do God's work, you will draw God's pay.

Yes, the voice of these unknown black bards sounds loud and clear in the midst of all the determined, uncompromising, and just struggles of all those who are the victims of injustice and oppression in this great land of ours. But it comes in a special way to the children of the slaves.

Let my children fight right on,
    O let my children fight right on;
Upon the mountain, down in the valley,
    You goin' to reap just what you sow!

We Are Climbin' Jacob's Ladder

We are climbin' Jacob's ladder,
   We are climbin' Jacob's ladder,
We are climbin' Jacob's ladder,
   Soldier of the cross.

Ev'ry round goes higher, higher,
   Soldier of the cross.

Sinner, do you love my Jesus?
   Soldier of the cross.

Rise, shine, give God the glory,
   Soldier of the cross.

And he dreamed, and behold a ladder set up on the earth, and the top of it reached to heaven: and behold the angels of God ascending and descending on it.—Genesis 28:12-13a

"We Are Climbin' Jacob's Ladder" is one of the moving songs of aspiration which the Negro slave singers bequeathed to the world. It is interesting to note the unique way in which the singers spiritualized their struggles under the yoke of slavery. They believed that their God was very definitely involved in their struggles and yearnings for freedom. Like Jacob, from whose marvelous experience they took this theme, they felt lonely and forsaken as they wandered in

83

the valley of slavery; but also like Jacob, they knew that they had encountered God along the weary and desolate way. They too envisioned a ladder let down to them from God, upon which they could climb. As they prayed, hoped, and aspired, they sang with great enthusiasm and determination: "We are climbing Jacob's ladder."

One cannot help but be moved with deep appreciation for these simple people, when he comes to share their sublime conviction that God had extended a ladder of sure help for them, even in the midst of their darkest night. Out of their black night of misery, fear, hurt, and sorrow, they could envision this heavenly ladder, upon which ascended angels of mourning and prayer, and from which descended God's hand of mercy and healing health. They felt themselves empowered by God's gracious hand, and could thus say as they strained forward, "Ev'ry round goes higher, higher." By faith they could look back and see that each round, though bitterly contested, had led them higher and higher.

The simple and beautiful words of this song suggest the slaves' determination to overcome their condition of slavery, but they also suggest mankind's perennial toils and struggles. All of us, at one time or another, have experienced this climbing of Jacob's ladder.

During my first year in seminary, after having pulled up stakes and gone some considerable distance from the old familiar surroundings, I found myself teaching students who were dropouts. They were working mothers and fathers, and were only able to attend night classes. I shall always remember the beautiful and meaningful manner in which these students, who were attempting under difficult conditions to complete their high school education, sang this song during one of our devotional periods. They had been toiling through the long, long day, victims of overwork and little pay. Yet they were trying determinedly to extricate themselves from their seemingly helpless and hopeless condition by attending school at night. This melody, rising upon the wings of their God-given voices, reverberated throughout the building: "We are climbin' Jacob's ladder; We are climbin' Jacob's ladder; . . . Every round goes higher, higher." It seemed to me that I heard other voices, thousands of voices, rising up from the cotton fields and sugar lands of the old South, echoing We have been struggling, striving, pressing, straining; yea, climbing across these years with you; we are still climbing. I knew then that this was the marching song, the battle cry, of the slaves. What more appropriate language could be employed to suggest our worthy ambitions and aspirations? In many ways, we too are climbing our Jacob's ladder.

Let us always keep in mind that the slave singers, in picturing their aspirations in terms of climbing Jacob's ladder, were thinking not only of their struggles up from slavery; but also of their deep inner spiritual and religious struggles. Here again we note the genius of the Negro spirituals. They almost always beautifully combined the two struggles, because for the slaves these struggles were ultimately inseparable. They were sure that by God's help they were steadily and resolutely climbing up out of the terrible and unbearable pit of sin and its consequences. Here in a deep spiritual sense they knew that they were climbing Jacob's ladder, with every round going higher, higher.

Truly, in these words the slave singers were bearing witness to the fact of sin, and to the fact that God's blessed angels of help always come to sustain and support the soul

85

in its aspirations to overcome even the power of sin. In another well-known song these singers expressed the same spirit of aspiration and expectation: "Lord, I want to be like Jesus in-a my heart."

Realizing that they were not climbing in their own strength, but surely because of the continued help of God, the unknown bards continued this beautiful and soul-stirring song; "Rise, shine, give God the Glory!" This declaration that they were climbing Jacob's ladder must never be understood as a thankless expression of pride and self-attainment; rather for them it was a joyful exultation in what God was doing in and through them. It was a jubilant and spontaneous expression of gratitude that they had come thus far by faith and by grace. So if by God's grace we know ourselves to be aspiring, climbing, reaching for, and even laying hold upon new spiritual heights, we too, must rise, shine, and give God the glory.

Nobody Knows de Trouble I See

Oh, nobody knows de trouble I see,
  Nobody knows but Jesus;
Nobody knows de trouble I see,
  Glory, hallelujah!

Sometimes I'm up, sometimes I'm down, oh, yes, Lord,
  Sometimes I'm almos' to the ground, oh, yes, Lord.
Although you see me goin' 'long so, oh, yes, Lord;
  I have my troubles here below, oh, yes, Lord.

Oh, nobody knows de trouble I see,
  Nobody knows but Jesus;
Nobody knows de trouble I see,
  Glory, hallelujah!

*My soul faintest for thy salvation: but I hope in thy word.
Mine eyes fail for thy word, saying, When wilt thou comfort
me? For I am become like a bottle in the smoke; yet do I
not forget thy statutes. How many are the days of thy servant? when wilt thou execute judgment on them that persecute me? The proud have digged pits for me, which are
not after they law. . . .*

*They had almost consumed me upon earth; but I forsook
not thy precepts.*—Psalm 119:81-85, 87

Here is perhaps one of the most sorrowful of all the great spirituals. One really has to hear it sung with all its touching effects in order to appreciate the depths which it sounds. It is also one of the most beautiful and artistic pieces of subtle protest. It is a cry out of the utter depths of loneliness and forsakenness.

Living beyond the boundaries of real vital concern is sung about again and again in the spirituals, perhaps because there are few experiences indeed that can more definitely break one's spirit than the feeling of being alone. And this feeling of living outside the real sympathy and care of others was so characteristic of the slave life.

Nobody knows the trouble I see. We must keep in mind that this spiritual, like most, is a community song. The slaves sought to console each other by saying that nobody who had not lived under the conditions of slavery could possibly know the trouble they knew. They were saying that no one could really empathize with them, unless he had walked the lonely and forsaken path with them.

I recall one lady trying to console another at the burial of her father. The consoler still had a mother living, and the sorrowing lady was burying her last parent. Thus she cried to her comforter in despair, "But you still have a mother." She was trying to say, "you can't know how I feel, until you walk where I am walking." It was in this spirit that the slaves burst forth in uncontrollable sorrow; "Oh, nobody knows. . . ." Is it any wonder that they were often overcome with emotionalism in their worship services?

They cried out from the depths of the human hell in which they were entrapped. "Nobody knows the trouble I see, nobody knows that I hurt like any other human being, and for the same reasons any other human being hurts.

88

Nobody knows or seems to understand that I love like any other human being, and therefore to have my children torn from my side leaves an empty place in my heart as surely as it would in any other human breast. Nobody knows that I have trials here below." How terrible that some do not have the capacity to understand this.

Again the black singers sang "Nobody Knows," because they knew that the people to whom they referred did not really care about them. The slaves' songs, we remember, were designed to convey a message to their masters as well as to comfort themselves. They knew that the pride, vanity, bigotry, lust, and greed of their masters had rendered them impervious to the cry of the slaves.

There is an unpublished song written by a wonderful singer I knew as a boy that aptly describes what I feel was in the hearts of the slaves as they sang their song:

> Nobody knows, and nobody cares,
> My heavy burden, nobody shares,
> Nobody cares even if I am ill
> Or if life's hardships have broken my will.

Nobody knows the trouble I see. Here the singers strike that deep religious note so evident in many of their noble songs: Nobody knows but Jesus. And Jesus knew, they felt, because, first of all, he was their fellow sufferer. "They crucified my Lord, and He never said a mumblin' word." They knew that they were not alone in their troubles. He was one with them. How comforting indeed it must have been to know that Jesus, who had walked the earthly path of sorrow and had overcome, now walked with them. Secondly, they knew that Jesus was aware of their troubles

89

because with him they had all the dignity of any of his other brothers. They believed in their hearts that with him even the least was the greatest. With him, they believed that the "angel" of the black child, even on the auction block, did "always behold the Father's face." Yes, with Jesus they were all of infinite worth. Nobody knows but Jesus, for he sees and cares. "My only comfort and my only stay, / Jesus walks by my side all the way!"

O Glory, Glory, Hallelujah!

O glory, glory, hallelujah!
   O glory, glory to that Lamb;
O glory, glory, hallelujah!
   Child of God, that's what I am!

He leadeth me into green pastures,
   Child of God, that's what I am!

He leadeth me beside still waters,
   Child of God, that's what I am!

See what love the Father has given us, that we should be called children of God; and so we are. . . . Beloved, we are God's children now; it does not yet appear what we shall be, but we know that when he appears we shall be like him, for we shall see him as he is.—I John 3:1-2.

But now thus saith the Lord that created thee, O Jacob, and he that formed thee, O Israel, Fear not: for I have redeemed thee, I have called thee by thy name; thou art mine. When thou passest through the waters, I will be with thee; and through the rivers, they shall not overflow thee: when thou walkest through the fire, thou shall not be burned neither shall the flame kindle upon thee.—Isaiah 43: 1-2

The writer of the beautiful and heartwarming and brief New Testament letter quoted above shared his faith with his readers. He bade them meditate on the good news that God out of his pure unmerited love for them had bestowed upon them the grace which allowed them to be called his children. What an occasion for rejoicing: We are children of the heavenly King here and now.

These blessed words of assurance found in this scripture passage must have come as trumpets of deliverance to the slave singers in their agony and forsakenness. Out of the wilderness of sorrow and darkness and oppression, their voices rang with joy akin to that of the biblical writers: "O glory, glory, hallelujah! Child of God, that's what I am!" These children of servitude expressed the unrivaled joy that comes to every heart that knows deep within that by God's amazing grace he is the child of God. This knowledge is the mighty fortress that has secured God's people everywhere; it has been the anchor of many storm-tossed souls. To feel that one is a child of a kind and loving God is all one needs to know.

The conviction that they were children of God gave the slaves a divine sense of security. Although insecure as slaves, they came to rejoice in the only lasting security that transient and frail humanity may know: I am a child of God, and if at any time I should fall, I will always fall into his loving arms. They must have often recalled also those blessed words of Isaiah: Thus saith Jehovah, . . . Fear not, for I have redeemed thee, I have called thee by thy name. . . . I will be with thee; . . . and the flame shall not burn thee."

The assurance that they were children of God gave them an indestructible sense of dignity. They were inspired to realize that they were indeed somebody, and that they always possessed worth and dignity before the God of the universe. Though circumstances clothed them in filth and

92

rags, and though they were housed in dungeons and subjected to all sorts of indignities, they knew that they were *somebody's* children, and that *somebody* loved and cared. It was this blessed assurance that kept the fires of freedom, hope, and determination aglow in their hearts. Exploited as they were on every hand, ostracized, rejected, and deprived, the slaves possessed a dignity that was truly invincible. They knew that in God's economy "all God's chillun got wings," and that someday, like his other children, they would rise upon the wings of a bright and glorious morning and leave the ugly dehumanizing conditions of slavery far behind. So in spite of all the assaults upon their dignity, the slave singers continued to sing this song with hope and assurance: "Child of God, that's what I am! O glory, glory to that Lamb!"

Through this undying sense of sonship the slaves knew that before the God who made them, all men were equal. They knew in their hearts that he was always a great arbitrator in the affairs of men, and that all men must finally stand before his presence. Sometimes, when their burdens were so heavy and the days so very dark and long, the slaves would sing for their masters:

> I'm goin' to tell God just how you treat me,
> When I lay my burdens down.

Yes, as children of God they knew that they possessed dignity and that this dignity would endure in spite of all that men could do to them.

The slaves' realization that they were children of God gave them a blessed sense of destiny. These sad and worn people of God believed in God, in his justice, and in his unfailing purpose. They knew themselves to be children of

God, and knew that their ultimate destiny was in God's hands. They believed that through his mercy they and their children were destined to be free. So sure were they that freedom would someday be theirs, they often escaped—in their imaginations—their awful world of slavery and lived for brief moments in the world of freedom:

> Free at last, free at last,
> Thank God Almighty,
> I'm free at last!

They knew that even though they were held in slavery, this was only man's temporary arrangement; for even then God was undoing this evil plot of man: My Lord, my Lord says he's gwineter rain down fire."

Let us always be reminded that the slaves not only believed that freedom was their ultimate destiny, but also believed that they were destined to live in the immediate presence of God. Perhaps no people have sung more gloriously of this hope than did they. After some warm and soul-stirring moment of worship, they often sang:

> Peter, go ring dem bells,
>   Peter, go ring dem bells,
> I heard from heab'n today!
>
> Gwine to heab'n some day!
>
> I'm so glad the other world
>   is not like dis!

I'm So Glad I Got My Religion in Time

I'm so glad I got my religion in time,
I'm so glad I got my religion in time,
I'm so glad I got my religion in time,
   O my Lord, O my Lord, what shall I do?

Make more room, Lord, in my heart for thee,
Make more room, Lord, in my heart for thee,
Make more room, Lord, in my heart for thee,
   O my Lord, O my Lord, what shall I do?

Run, sinner, run and hunt you an hidin' place,
Run, sinner, run and hunt you an hidin' place,
Run, sinner, run and hunt you an hidin' place,
   O my Lord, O my Lord, what shall I do?

How shall we escape, if we neglect so great salvation?—
Hebrews 2:3.

Today if ye will hear his voice, harden not your hearts.—
Hebrews 3:7b-8a.

The weary slaves who yielded their lives in thankful response to the love of God found in him such immeasurable joy and peace that they could but marvel that they had waited so long for such a glorious blessing. They realized that this wonderful, rich, and full life in God had been available to them all the time: and yet they were so unaware of its possibilities. They had so long refused this marvelous free gift of God, which they described in the song as religion. They realized that all the time they were fleeing from God he was pursuing them and offering to them this most precious gift. What if they had waited too late? What if God's amazing grace had not overtaken them in time? What if the harvest had passed and they had not been saved? It was against this background of thinking, this sense of time running out, that the slaves sang out: "I'm so glad I've got my religion in time." They were so glad that this deep love had come into their poor poverty-stricken lives before it was everlastingly too late. What joys they would have missed, what peaceful hours they would have forfeited, what blessed assurance would have passed them by. But now they shout out of hearts overflowing with gratitude, "I'm so glad, yes, so very glad, I got my religion in time." Like one who finds himself saved from some impending danger, they sang out with immeasurable joy, "in time, just in time."

This feeling that one turns to God barely in time (and here the poor unlearned slaves spoke so truly of the Christian faith) is one of the great truths of religious experience. The psalmist said, "As for me, my feet were almost gone; my steps had well nigh slipped" (Psalm 73:2). The blessed apostle Paul, who was finally laid hold upon by the risen Savior, always felt that the hour of his turning was oh so very late. "Like one born out of season," he often said. Augustine, whose heart was so long divided and whose will so woefully weak, lamented when once he had given himself completely to his Lord, "Too late did I love thee; thou wert with me, but I was not with Thee." He felt that somehow, out of God's abounding mercy, he had been saved just before it was too late. Kierkegaard says in his *Purity of Heart:* "When remorse awakens concern whether it be in youth, or in the old, it is always at the eleventh hour. It does not have much time at its disposal for it is the eleventh hour." Francis Thompson, in his *Hound of Heaven,* speaks of his tardiness in realizing the presence and the persistent pursuit of his Lord. He realized all too late that Christ was pursuing him all the time, but he was oblivious of his presence. When they sang, "I'm so glad I got my religion in time," the slaves truly expressed their deep feeling of gratitude for the abounding grace of God, which is so characteristic of all the saints.

"Make more room, Lord, in my heart for Thee," the bards continued to sing. They were not satisfied just to know that they had been snatched as "a brand from the burning" and had been claimed by God, but they would have their Savior completely possess them. Every faithful child of God knows something of the yearning and longing to be completely filled and controlled by God. But he also knows something of the great surge of those things which would crowd God out of his life. The slaves knew that there is just never enough room in our hearts for God and all of our selfish ambitions. And so we may all truly join with the slaves in this prayer, Make some room, Lord, in my heart for thee. We, like them, must ask God to widen our hearts and to do for us by his grace what we cannot do for ourselves.

Finally, these singers, who like John Bunyan's pilgrim felt in their souls that they had barely fled the burning city in time, turned to their complacent sinner brother and cried with a dramatic sense of urgency, "Run, sinner, run and

97

hunt you an hiding place." They had come in their own lives to know that they indeed had a home and security in the Rock. But their sympathy and concern went out to those who knew not this security. I realized as a lad how this concern for those "without the ark of safety" possessed the heart of my elders. They not only pled with the sinner, but they wept with and for the sinner. I can almost hear those cries how that went up from the crowded church during the traditional revivals, "Run, sinner, run and hunt you a hiding place." This is the terrible sense of urgency which they felt, and which we hear in their song.

It may be that this concern for the unsaved was a bit too limited. But oh how much we need a passion and concern for the lost and drifting lives today. We must surely interpret salvation in wider and more complete terms than the Negro slaves. But Christ's church must always be conscious of this sense of urgency. It must be the proclaiming, seeking, and searching church, for it is always the eleventh hour for all of God's children.

I Couldn't Hear Nobody Pray

An' I couldn't hear nobody pray, O Lord,
　I couldn't hear nobody pray, O Lord,
O 'way down yonder by myself,
　An' I couldn't hear nobody pray.

Chilly waters! I couldn't hear nobody pray.
　In de Jordan! I couldn't hear nobody pray.
Crossin' over! I couldn't hear nobody pray.
　Into Canaan! I couldn't hear nobody pray. O Lord!

In de valley! I couldn't hear nobody pray.
　On my knees! I couldn't hear nobody pray.
Wid my burden! I couldn't hear nobody pray.
　An' my Savior! I couldn't hear nobody pray. O
Lord!

Hallelujah! I couldn't hear nobody pray.
　Troubles over! I couldn't hear nobody pray.
In de Kingdom! I couldn't hear nobody pray.
　Wid my Jesus! I couldn't hear nobody pray. O
Lord!

My God, my God, why hast thou forsaken me?—Matthew
27:46b

There is a great chasm fixed between us; no one from our

99

*side who wants to reach you can cross it, and none may
pass from your side to us.*—Luke 16:26 NEB

This truly great spiritual touches a depth of human experience that only a few others can rival. In it the sensitive
soul can feel all the terrifying sorrow, sadness, and loneliness that the conditions of slavery heaped upon the slaves.
Perhaps their sorrowful souls could not have found a more
adequate expression for the utter loneliness and heaviness
of heart which they were experiencing than this one, which
says that in their hopes and ambitions to be free they were
indeed alone, that even in their prayers they felt all alone.
"O 'way down yonder by myself, an' I couldn't hear nobody
pray." What a dark and gloomy picture of life's condition!
Here I am, on my knees, talking with mankind's common
Father and praying a prayer expressing mankind's common
dream, and yet there is not another of his children who will
join me in prayer. It seems to me that the slave singers were
saying that not only were they so far down in the valley of
separation that they could hear no one else pray, but also
that they were so far down in this valley of sorrow and
tears that no one else could even hear them pray.

There is, however, another side of this picture of the
tragic state of isolation and loneliness to which this great
spiritual may well address itself. The singers sang most
eloquently and pathetically of their own state of loneliness,
but their song was meant to remind their captors that they
too dwelt in a valley. While the black man and his children
have been alienated and isolated by visible and invisible
walls—both legal and illegal—so have the white man and his
children been isolated and alienated by walls; of their prej-

udice, their false sense of superiority, their pride, and their vanity. Both black and white have been way down yonder in the valley by themselves. The one has been forced to remain in the valley by himself, and has not been able to hear anyone praying because he has been too far removed. The other has forced himself to dwell alone in his valley, and he has not been able to hear anyone beyond the valley praying because his ears have become deaf through indifference and callousness. Being held in the valley has muffled and smothered the prayers of the one, while the one holding him there has hardened his heart until he has lost the sensitivity to respond. For one be left alone in the valley, even in prayers, in hopes, or in dreams, is tragic indeed, but for one to grow insensitive and deaf to the cries of those who shout for release from the valley is far more tragic.

The slave singers knew what it meant to dwell in the dark and dismal valley of trouble and sorrow. Also, by the grace of God they knew what it meant to be alone, yet surely and truly not alone. Their message of assurance resounded from their valley, yes, way down yonder in their valley, "On my knees, I couldn't hear nobody pray. With my burden and my Savior." Even in their haunting loneliness they experienced another Presence with them, saying, "I will never leave thee, nor forsake thee" (Hebrews 13:5c). Sometimes their burdens were so hard to bear; yet, as they bore their burdens, they encountered along the way a burden-bearing companion who says to all who turn to him: "My yoke is easy, and my burden is light." They came to share the blessed presence of Jesus, who knew loneliness as no other, who even on the cross, forsaken by all men, cried unto God: "My God, my God, why hast thou forsaken me?" We rejoice that in spite of all the pathos and sorrow

101

running through this song there is still that note of radiant hope, hope born in the darkness, and yet hope bursting forth in song even in the night. "Hallelujah! . . . Troubles over! . . . In the Kingdom! . . . With my Jesus." Such was the faith, hope, assurance, and determination of the slaves. May it be that in our frustrations, loneliness, separation, and brokenness we too shall truly find a common hope shining through all the darkness that engulfs us. May we live in the assurance that together, sharing in each other's worthy prayers, "We shall overcome someday."

This song and its message must not be left in the past because it so aptly describes the continuous isolation and alienation of the children of the slaves. These children are still striving and struggling to extricate themselves from their lonesome valley. They are asking to become a real and living part of the mainstream of our great society. This terrifying valley that separates blacks from whites is nothing new. It has always been there. It is true that many cry about the great division in our society today, but the truth is, blacks and whites have been shouting to each other across this valley of separation from the beginning of slavery until now. They have not been able to hear or to understand each other. They have not been speaking the same language. Justice, freedom, fulfillment have not meant the same thing for all.

It is true that here and there along the way a few children of the slaves have managed to escape the dark and lonely ghetto and blend their voices in prayer with those beyond the valley. But the majority have remained nameless and unheard in their ghetto. I have come to realize that the ghetto is not only a place, but also a state of human existence. To live in the ghetto is to be trapped in the valley of isolation with all the lines of communication down. To be in the ghetto is to be void of aspirations for oneself or for one's children. It means to see the sun of hope going down without any feelings that it will rise tomorrow. To live in the ghetto of human experience is to be dehumanized and depersonalized, and made to become the victim of one's own despising. Indeed, to live in a valley like this where no one seems to care and where no sympathetic hand of help is extended is to be way down yonder by oneself, where one can hear nobody pray, and where no one shares one's prayers, or hopes, or ambitions. Lou Rawls very fittingly describes this life in the yonder valley and the ghetto when he sings, "I was born on a dead-end street."

Steal Away to Jesus

Steal away, steal away,
    Steal away to Jesus!
Steal away, steal away home,
    I ain't got long to stay here!

My Lord, he calls me,
    He calls me by de thunder;
De trumpet sounds within-a my soul:
    I ain't got long to stay here.

Dark clouds arisin',
    Poor sinners stand a-tremblin';
De trumpet sounds within-a my soul:
    I ain't got long to stay here.

Come unto me, all ye that labour and are heavy laden, and I will give you rest. Take my yoke upon you, and learn of me; for I am meek and lowly in heart: and ye shall find rest unto your souls. For my yoke is easy, and my burden is light.—Matthew 11:28-30.

I go to prepare a place for you, And if I go and prepare a place for you, I will come again, and receive you unto myself; that where I am, there ye may be also.—John 14:2b-4.

My voice shalt thou hear in the morning, O Lord; in the morning will I direct my prayer unto thee, and will look up.—Psalm 5:3.

"Steal Away" is one of the best-known spirituals. Most students of Negro folk songs believe that this song represented a call to worship by our slaves. It was used to announce their secret meetings. As the slaves worked in the fields, one group would begin singing "steal away," and the group in an adjacent field would pick up the song. This process would continue until the song had reached the ears of numerous slaves.

I also feel that since the "underground railroad" played such an important part in the lives of the slaves, this beautiful song may have been used to announce the arrival of the underground train, so the slaves could prepare themselves to steal away.

Whatever conditions may have suggested this spiritual, we can easily understand some of its deeper meanings for the slaves. Slavery was for them an unbearable condition, and it was only by God's grace that they developed the uncanny ability to steal away from it all. They could always find temporary refuge and gain added strength and endurance in such a song.

Not only was the singing of the song a stealing away from it all, but also the precious assembly to which it called them was for them a very meaningful escape. Alone with themselves in the presence of Jesus they knew themselves to be free. For the presence of Jesus transmutes any outward ugly condition. Here they found moments of freedom in the midst of their eternity of slavery. That their meetings were so spirited and charged with emotionalism it should not cause us to wonder, for these worship services represented for them a stealing away home to Jesus. They found in them one of life's beautiful resting places.

106

Though the slaves were enraptured by these precious moments in the presence of Jesus, they knew that they didn't have long to stay there. They must prepare to go back into the battle of real life as it was.

This song also reminds us of the deep spiritual sensitivity of the slave singers. Even in the midst of slavery and its unspeakable conditions they were ever conscious of God's presence. God was all about them. He was truly their "refuge and strength, and a very present help in trouble." So near was God to them, and so sensitive were they to his presence that they could hear his voice in all of nature. They could hear his voice in the trumpet call of the thunder, they could see him in the flashing of the lightning and in the rising of the dark clouds, and even in the bending of the green trees. This voice that they heard in the various aspects of nature was no general voice, but a trumpet call within each soul. The voice was so personal and so summoned souls into the presence of their Lord that as poor sinners they always stood trembling. "My Lord, he calls me, . . . The trumpet sounds within-a my soul."

Finally, in this song the slaves give voice to a deep sense of alienation. The voice of their Lord calling them assured them that they must steal away home. I feel that there were at least three ways in which slaves referred to home. First, they referred to home as a state of freedom. There was nothing that they hoped and longed for any more than to escape the chains of servitude. Slavery for them meant being in a far country a long way from home. So all their prayers and all their hopes were directed to God that he would lead them into a land of freedom.

Second, those noble singers struck a true religious note when they spoke of home. For many of them had found

107

their homes where Christian saints across the ages had found theirs, no matter what the outward circumstances of their lives; in the presence and love of Jesus. "Where I am there ye may be also." In his presence they found rest for the weary and a home for the pilgrim of sorrow.

O Jesus, my Saviour, on Thee I'll depend,
    When troubles am near me, you'll be my true friend.
Oh, laden with trouble an' burdened wid grief,
    To Jesus in secret I'll go for relief.

Third, when the slaves spoke of home, they were thinking of their eternal home. Sometimes the slave was so burdened with the load of slave life that he would sing, "I'm so glad this world is not my home." Slave singers were always at their best when they sang of their final home. For they truly believed that there God would make it up to them. At home with him the frustrations and the sorrows and the troubles of slavery would be left far behind. God's heaven was very near and very real for them. So this beautiful song was employed most often in commending a dying soul to the arms of Jesus.

It surely does not overtax the imagination to envision a band of slave saints gathered about the bedside of a dying comrade. In the final moments of their vigil they watch as his soul moves out toward the Jordan, accompanying it to the water's edge, they send this soul out across the deep to the beautiful tune of "Steal away, steal away to Jesus. Steal away home, I ain't got long to stay here."

Let Us Break Bread Togedder on Our Knees

Let us break bread togedder on our knees,
   Let us break bread togedder on our knees,
When I fall on my knees wid my face to de risin'
      sun,
   Oh, Lord, hab mercy on me.

Let us drink wine togedder on our knees,
   Let us drink wine togedder on our knees,
When I fall on my knees wid my face to de risin'
      sun,
   Oh, Lord, hab mercy on me.

Let us praise God togedder on our knees,
   Let us praise God togedder on our knees,
When I fall on my knees wid my face to de risin'
      sun,
   Oh, Lord, hab mercy on me.

And it came to pass, as he sat at meat with them, he took bread, and blessed it, and brake, and gave to them. And their eyes were opened, and they knew him; and he vanished out of their sight. . . .

And they told what things were done in the way, and how he was known of them in breaking of bread.—Luke 24:30-31, 35.

This is one of the rare songs of the slaves that speak of communion. It is a most beautiful call to Holy Communion and blessed fellowship. It seems strange that such an arresting call to communion should come from the souls of those very people who knew so well what it meant to be left out. But miraculous as it may seem, this song plumbs the depths of the real meaning of Holy Communion when it gives this simple invitation in love to all who would hear and respond, "Let us break bread together."

The slave singers began with one of the most essential elements in the Communion service, the emphasis on the invitation to oneness. At the Lord's Table there is no room for exclusiveness, pride of position, status, or favor. There is no appealing to the worthy or the unworthy, but to mankind, without the thought of excluding any. For the slaves, there was no opposite of the "us" when they came to the communion table, only a simple call to all who would come into this simple and unadorned fellowship to "break bread together."

To understand this call as it was sung by the slaves and to really enter into it one must emphasize and underscore "together" as well as "us." In emphasizing the breaking of the bread and the drinking of the wine "together," the slaves recaptured the spirit of that first upper room drama. For had not the Lord, theirs and ours said in that room on that fateful night: "Take this and divide it among yourselves," and "Drink ye all of it"? And did he not give a piece of bread even to Judas the traitor? And did he not say, "Where two or three are gathered together in my name, there am I in the midst of them"? And what else does communion mean if it does not call us away from our state of brokenness and separateness to a togetherness in Christ? It calls us away from our blackness and whiteness, from our pride and vanity from our selfishness and exclusiveness to a oneness in loving service.

This marvelous song of the slaves calls us not only to break bread and to drink wine together, but to do so on our knees. Let us ever keep in mind the very special emphasis which those singers placed on the expression "on our knees." They would not dare break the most sacred bread and drink the lifegiving wine except in a spirit of deep and reverent humility. They could also say, "we are not worthy even to gather up the crumbs from thy table." Surely they felt that they must bow on their knees before God, the giver of the bread and wine, and the giver of Jesus, whose body and blood are represented by the broken bread and the blood-red wine. But I am also convinced that the slave singers offer even greater insight into the meaning of communion as they call us to our knees, for they were not only calling for humility before God, but for humility before one another. This indeed is the glory, wonder, beauty, and miracle of the blessed communion. Those who would come to the Lord's Table are called to bow before him with one another. We are hereby called to recognize and to acknowledge the humanity and the divinity in each other. It may not take too much grace for the average soul to bow before the God who gives all and upon whom he is so dependent, but how rich one must be in heavenly grace in order to be able to sincerely bow alongside a poor soul who demands all and can give nothing in return, with one so low he cannot even offer gratitude in return for loving kindness. It may not require too much to join "with angels and archangels and

111

all the company of heaven" in praising God, but it requires miraculous grace to join with the despised, the rejected, the brokenhearted, and the dropouts of society in building up one another.

Yet this is the very miracle of the blessed communion. It means the rich bowing down with the poor; the learned with the unlearned; the clean with the filthy; the master with the slave; the privileged with the deprived; the white with the black; and the black with the white.

"On our knees" is symbolic not only of our readiness to serve God but also of our readiness to serve the least among his children. We marvel that the greatest among men on that solemn occasion arose from the table and girded himself with a towel and, pouring water in a basin, like the true servant he was, he washed the feet of his most unworthy disciple.

What marvelous insights the untutored slaves shared with us as they sang, "When I fall on my knees with my face to the rising sun." They always somehow found the grace to face the rising sun. They may have been on their knees, but they always faced the sun of a new day with hope and anticipation. The blessed communion, when shared in the true spirit, will always turn our faces toward the rising sun. We fall on our knees with the slave singers, with our faces too having been turned from darkness to light, from despair to hope, from bondage to freedom, from sin to a sense of forgiveness, from hate to love, from selfishness to self-giving, from pride and vanity to humility, from sorrow to joy, from brokeness to wholeness, from alienation to a glorious oneness in Christ, from the mountaintop of inspiration to the valley of humble service: Yes, we turn from

the haunting and gnawing nightmare of our own concerns
to the glory of the cross of Christ and his suffering children.

> Let us praise God togedder on our knees.
> When I fall on my knees wid my face to de risin' sun,
> Oh, Lord, hab mercy if you please.

Lord, I Want to Be a Christian

Lord, I want to be a Christian in-a my heart, in-a my heart;
   Lord, I want to be a Christian in-a my heart.
In-a my heart, in-a my heart,
   Lord, I want to be a Christian in-a my heart.

Lord, I want to be more holy in-a my heart, in-a my heart;
   Lord, I want to be more holy in-a my heart.

I don't want to be like Judas in-a my heart, in-a my heart;
   I don't want to be like Judas in-a my heart.

I just want to be like Jesus in-a my heart, in-a my heart;
   I just want to be like Jesus in-a my heart.

As the hart panteth after the water brooks, so panteth my soul after thee, O God.—Psalm 42:1

Blessed are they which do hunger and thirst after righteousness: for they shall be filled.—Matthew 5:6

This spiritual expresses the deep hunger and longings of the human soul. The slave singers had tasted the Lord and had found him to be good, so they sought a closer fellowship with him. If we would understand this prayer of the slaves, we must hear them say that the yearning for more love and more Christlikeness springs from their innermost being.

115

There is a calling out from the very depth of their lives for more and more love, more and more holiness.

They are asking that the very center of their being be indwelt by the love of Christ. They would have his love permeate their total life. How truly did these singers put it, for it is for the very heart of man that our living Christ is ever asking. It is the very center of the soul of man that cries out to be filled with the divine spirit. This longing for Christ, this desire to be completely possessed by him has been expressed in many ways across the centuries, but perhaps never more simple and yet never more profoundly said than in these precious words: "Lord, I want to be more loving in my heart," and "Lord, I want to be like Jesus in my heart."

This great spiritual, like many others, must have strengthened many poor souls in their private devotion. How wonderful it must have been to be awakened in the morning to face a new day with this song surging from the very depths of their souls. "Lord, the one prayer that I would make today is that I may genuinely be a Christian; not that I may wear the name of Christ, but that I may be given the grace to be wholly like Jesus in my heart of hearts. May the very wellsprings of my life be pure and clean. May His precious spirit, like the sun, flood my whole inner life banishing all ill will, all unloveliness, all untruthfulness, all callousness. Keep my life free from sin and my heart pure within."

"Lord, I want to be more holy in my heart." Here the slave expresses his deep desire to feel and to know that he had been completely set apart for God's service. He knew that if he were to be holy, God would have to make him holy.

116

Breathe on me, Breath of God,
    Fill me with life anew,
That I may love what thou dost love,
    And do what thou wouldst do.

"Lord, I don't want to be like Judas in my heart." This petition sounds a warning to every professed follower of Christ. There is always the possibility that he may play the part of Judas; and how truly did the slave singers sing when they warned that this spirit of Judas lurked near every heart. They knew how strongly they would resist the spirit of betrayal, and yet how easily they could drift into the path of being a traitor. They often felt this spirit of Judas in their hearts just as we do, and so they prayed passionately: "Lord, I don't want to be like Judas in my heart. I don't want to follow you halfheartedly and then somewhere along the line utterly betray you. Keep me true, pure, and holy in my heart."

I just want to be like Jesus in my heart. This is the supreme desire of the faithful, to bear the stamp of Jesus upon his heart. Like Paul they wanted to "know him, and the power of his resurrection, and the fellowship of his sufferings."

I just want to be like Jesus in my heart. Fannie Crosby leads us also upon this quest in some of her songs:

Let me love thee more and more . . .
Till my soul is lost in love.

Draw me nearer, nearer, nearer, blessed Lord,
To thy precious, bleeding side.

117

Lord, that all other desires, all other ambitions should be completely subordinate to this one all prevailing obsession: "I just want to be like Jesus in my heart." Just like Jesus, "We are already the children of God; . . . but . . . when he shall appear, we shall be like him."

Were You There When They Crucified My Lord?

Were you there when they crucified my Lord?
  Were you there, when they crucified my Lord?
Oh! Sometimes it causes me to tremble, tremble, tremble.
  Were you there when they crucified my Lord?

Were you there when they nailed him to the tree?
  Were you there when they nailed him to the tree?
Oh! Sometimes it causes me to tremble, tremble, tremble.
  Were you there when they nailed him to the tree?

Were you there when they pierced him in the side?
  Were you there when they pierced him in the side?
Oh! Sometimes it causes me to tremble, tremble, tremble.
  Were you there when they pierced him in the side?

Were you there when the sun refused to shine?
  Were you there when the sun refused to shine?
Oh! Sometimes it causes me to tremble, tremble, tremble.
  Were you there when the sun refused to shine?

Were you there, when they laid him in the tomb?
  Were you there, when they laid him in the tomb?
Oh! Sometimes it causes me to tremble, tremble, tremble.
  Were you there when they laid him in the tomb?

119

. . . Seeing they crucify to themselves the Son of God afresh, and put him to an open shame.—Hebrews 6:6b.

I am crucified with Christ: nevertheless I live; yet not I, but Christ liveth in me.—Galatians 2:20a.

The writer of that masterful sermon known as the letter to the Hebrews reminded his readers of the most sobering truth; that it is always possible, even for the followers of Christ, to crucify him anew for themselves. What a frightening possibility this is. Yet even you and I can crucify our Lord anew for ourselves.

The Negro slave singers put this same truth in dramatic, moving, and picturesque language, as they raised the startling question, "Were you there when they crucified my Lord?" With vivid imagination they invite all of us to walk with them to Calvary, and there in the presence of the Crucifixion scene bid us to examine our hearts. "Did you really have any part in this?" they ask. "Are you completely innocent?" Then while we are trying to absolve ourselves of any guilt, they make haste to confess their own involvement in this terrible crime. "Oh! Sometimes," they say, "it causes me to tremble, tremble, tremble." The slaves were horrified to know that they were somehow involved in the death of the Lord.

The suffering and misery and anguish of body and soul that characterized the lives of these slaves no doubt gave them that unusual and sublime ability to identify with our Lord in his suffering. His suffering and loneliness were not too foreign to them. Their terrible and undeserved misery and suffering gave them deep insight into and sympathy with the awful and undeserving suffering of our Lord. They knew out of their own fresh, hot, and bitter experiences what it meant to bear in their own bodies those innocent scars. The question "What evil has he done?" was very real to them. They knew themselves to be crucified every day both in body and in soul. Yet what evil had they done?

Whatever parallel these singers may have drawn between their suffering and that of their Lord, they recognized that theirs was as nothing when compared with his. They were always deeply sensitive to the terrible crime inflicted upon them, and yet they considered it as nothing when compared with mankind's terrible crime against their Savior.

> This World treat you mean, Lord,
> Treats me mean too. . . .

> Sweet little Jesus boy,
> We didn't know who you was.

Those lonely and burdened singers knew also that the crucified Lord was one who could understand and enter into their sorrows. They not only identified themselves with his suffering, but also identified themselves with their Lord's sympathies. They knew that only he who could say in death, "Father, into thy hands I commend my spirit," could also commend their souls to God.

"Oh! Sometimes it causes me to tremble, tremble, tremble," because in sympathy and sorrow and loneliness and forsakenness I was there. I know what he went through because I have met him in the deep, dark valley of pain and sorrow, and there we have joined hands and hearts.

I am not at all convinced that the slave singers were able to think in a logical manner of their kinship to all mankind in this terrible crime, but it does seem to me that the

121

implications are indeed here. Is not this song a confession that the slaves knew that they had it in their own hearts to commit such a crime?

It was envy, hatred, greed, prejudice, pride, lust, selfishness, and vanity that led to the death of Jesus. The slave singers were acquainted with all of these deep down in their hearts. They sometimes felt that had they really been there, they would have been allied with the powers and forces that sought to destroy their Lord. This song suggests the exceeding sinfulness of all men's hearts. To think upon the terrible wickedness of men's hearts, and of their own hearts, caused the slaves to tremble, tremble, tremble. They could well say to us: If you really want to know what is in man, if you really want to know something of man's awful proneness to sin, come with me! If you want to know the depth to which mankind can sink, come with me! Do you see that lonely bleeding figure hanging there? If you can bear it, look at the agony on his face, feel his deep rejection, enter into his loneliness, and share if you can his immeasurable pain and sorrow. There is the best and noblest that God and all the ages could produce, and yet see what we have all done to him. Oh! Sometimes, indeed, it causes me to tremble, tremble, tremble. Were you there when they crucified my Lord?

To the profoundly imaginative and creative minds of the slaves, the suffering and agony on Calvary were greatly unlike anything that the world had ever known. Somehow they came to know in their own hearts that the infinite God was truly identified in this terrible suffering. They knew that on that "old rugged cross" God's suffering love, which streams from eternity, was brought to a focal point. At Golgotha they felt that they were standing in the presence

122

of the "Lamb that was slain from the foundation of the world." Who would not tremble, standing in the presence of such a dramatic revelation of holy love? Certainly one would tremble all the more when made to realize that even he could have helped to perpetrate such a crime, and that at the same time he is joyfully a beneficiary of this precious death and suffering: He has indeed been bought with a price. And what a price! Oh! Sometimes it causes me to tremble, tremble, tremble.

There is indeed life and hope and joy and peace in this cross to which those singers would have us look, but their song also suggests a solemn note of warning. For Christ's cross is ever near us, we cannot escape it. We cannot escape our involvement in it. Were you there? The correct answer is always yes. Wash our hands as often as we may, the blood is still there. The question is always there: Shall we approach the cross with thanksgiving and a trembling sense of indebtedness as the slaves did, and thereby go forth in its strength to take up our own crosses and follow him; or shall we remain insensitive, indifferent, and careless and thus crucify our Lord anew? For wherever human misery, suffering, sorrow, hurt, and harm come even to the least of his children, he is always there. The whole matter becomes not only the question "Were you there?" but also, in the face of human suffering the questions: "Are you there?" and "Will you always be there?" To be indifferent toward, to neglect, to forget, or to spurn one of his little ones is to do so unto him. There is always the frightening danger that we crucify our Lord anew even though we never raise our hands against him. Oh, black and unknown bards, we are eternally indebted to you for being so very sensitive to and horrified by the suffering and agony of our Lord, and for

123

reminding us in such piercing phrases that every day we face that terrible and frightening possibility of crucifying our Lord anew for ourselves. You have taught us to know that we were indeed there when they crucified our Lord. And surely, "It causes us to tremble, tremble, tremble," as we acknowledge in sorrow and repentance that we were there.

Dere's Plenty Good Room

There's plenty good room, dere's plenty good room,
   Plenty good room in my Father's kingdom.
Plenty good room, plenty good room,
   Just choose your seat and sit down.

O brother, don't stay away, O sister, don't stay away,
   For my Lord says dere is room enough,
Room enough in Heaven for us all,
   My Lord says dere's room enough, so don't stay away.

*And James and John, the sons of Zebedee, came unto him,
saying, Master, we would that thou shouldest do for us
whatsoever we shall desire. And he said unto them, What
would ye that I should do for you? They said unto him,
Grant unto us that we may sit, one on thy right hand, and
the other on thy left hand, in thy glory.*

*But Jesus said unto them, Ye know not what ye ask:
can ye drink of the cup that I drink of? and be baptized with
the baptism that I am baptized with?*

*And they said unto him, We can. And Jesus said unto
them, Ye shall indeed drink of the cup that I drink of:
and with the baptism that I am baptized withal shall ye
be baptized: But to sit on my right hand and on my left
hand is not mine to give: but it shall be given to them for
whom it is prepared.—Mark 10:35-40*

*Let not your heart be troubled: ye believe in God, believe
also in me. In my Father's house are many mansions: if it*

125

*were not so, I would have told you. I go to prepare a place
for you.—John 14: 1-2*

*Go out quickly into the streets and lanes of the city, and
bring in hither the poor, and the mained, and the halt, and
the blind. And the servant said, Lord, it is done as thou
hast commanded, and yet there is room. And the Lord said
unto the servant, Go out into the highways and hedges,
and compel them to come in, that my house may be filled.—*
    Luke 14:21b-33

In this beautiful expression "Dere's plenty good room,"
the slave singers even more fittingly than they knew gave
voice to the very nature of God's kingdom. This most
penetrating insight came to them in the midst of the most
crowded conditions of life. It could have been that the
lack of ample room in their living quarters suggested to them
that in the economy of God there is always ample room for
all. They knew what it meant to be cheated out of their
rightful place in human society; they knew perhaps better
than any other people what it meant to be pushed into one
of life's cramped little corners. Perhaps the sight of their
little overcrowded cabins in contrast with the spacious "big
house" gave them the spiritual insight to envision the vast-
ness of God's providence. They knew in their own hearts,
as they experienced the fullness of God's love, that he did
not deal with his children in a mean or stingy way. So they
could sing as they drew upon his most precious promises:
"My Lord says dere's room enough for us all." How true
indeed was what they sang: for life's crowded conditions are due many times, not only to a general lack of

126

space, but also to the fact that someone is occupying more than his rightful share.

The singers also remind us that in God's economy, where life counts the most, there are vast spheres where there is plenty good room. God revealed to the humble slaves that in lowly paths of service for one's fellowman, there is plenty good room. In such lowly service they found their truest freedom. Such quest for service is reflected in the words of this verse they sometimes sang joyfully:

> Keep so busy workin' for my Jesus,
> Keep so busy workin' for my Jesus,
>   I ain't got time to die.
>
> Feedin' the po', I'm workin' for my Jesus,
> Feedin' the po', I'm workin' for my Jesus,
>   I ain't got time to die.

They suggested also that in the lonely path of sorrow, there is plenty good room. Yes, in this sphere one does not have to push or scramble for a place, for here with God's sorrowing children there is plenty good room. This has been the testimony not only of slave saints, but of all the true saints of God. There are always plenty sorrowful and broken hearts to bind: and living to help bind up broken hearts is sharing in the plenitude of the Father's kingdom.

> Comforting the sad, I'm working for my Jesus,
> Comforting the sad, I'm working for my Jesus,
>   I ain't got time to die.

The slaves knew from their own bitter experience that there is always plenty good room in the dark and forbidding path of suffering. As they walked together through their

127

dark valley of suffering, they comforted each other as they sang: "You pray for me, and I'll pray for you." They also knew in their own hearts something of the unfettered joy that can come to the soul that has developed the spiritual capacity to enter into the suffering of others. These blessed children of suffering had come to consider themselves brothers of all who suffer. In this path they knew, as all true sympathizers know, there is plenty good room.

Sooner or later the road from Jerusalem to Jericho will pass by our doors as well. Human suffering and misery and agony and pain and defeat and frustration and brokenness will surround us, and blessed are we when we have eyes that see, and ears that hear, and hearts that respond.

The beautiful and soul-stirring songs of the slaves, which represented their philosophy of life, represented also one of the great miracles of human history. For it was to these simple and burdened souls, without station or rank, that God revealed the spirit of his kingdom. They the disinherited had inherited his kingdom, in which there was plenty good room "Blessed are the poor in spirit; for theirs is the kingdom of heaven."

It was always with ecstatic joy that these weary and burdened souls sang of the wideness in God's mercies. In the very midst of their overcrowded quarters and in the face of the fact that they were vagabonds tossed and driven, they came to share that blessed assurance that the doors to the Father's house stand open for all his children. Heaven revealed to their seeking souls that God had no "special children." As a matter of fact, they knew that no one was worthy of his great invitation, but because he loved all, he invited all. In him they knew were no ranks or stations, neither was there slave or master, black or white; but because of his

128

unconditional love for all, he had provided room in abundance for all. No one need stay away.

Surely many of the slaves who died in this faith passed on to the Father's eternal house with that glorious word of our Lord before them: "In my Father's house are many mansions. . . . I go to prepare a place for you" (John 14: 2a, c.)

We may all thank God today that through this simple, beautiful, and childlike song of those unidentified slaves, our own horizons continue to be pushed back. Through them we continue to be chastened in our narrowness, prejudice, and bigotry. Through this song we are reminded that out there with God is an all-inclusiveness, a fullness of life. There is indeed "plenty good room."

I'm Noways Weary an' I'm Noways Tired

I'm noways weary an' I'm noways tired, hallelujah!
I expect to shout "O glory!" when de world's on fire.
O glory, hallelujah!

Better days are comin', better days are comin', hallelujah!

Members don't get weary, members don't get weary, hallelujah!

Keep yo' lamp trimmed an' a-burnin', keep yo' lamp trimmed an' a-burnin', hallclujah!

But one thing I do, forgetting what lies behind and straining forward to what lies ahead, I press on toward the goal for the prize of the upward call of God in Christ Jesus.—
  Philippians 3:13b RSV

Ye are all the children of light, and the children of the day: we are not of the night, nor of darkness. Therefore let us not sleep, as do others; but let us watch and be sober, For they that sleep sleep in the night; and they that be drunken are drunken in the night. But let us who are of the day, be sober, putting on the breast plate of faith and love; and for an helmet, the hope of salvation.—I Thessalonians 5:5-8

Let us run with patience the race that is set before us.—
  Hebrews 12:1b

131

Many of the great moments of my childhood occurred in the old-fashioned class meetings in which many former slaves participated. Here each one gave his testimony; and there was always a note of determination and resolution in all of them. The testimonies usually closed with words like these: "I'm determined to hold out to he end"; "I never expect to turn back, the best is before me"; "If I see you no more, I'll meet you on the other shore." These were indeed high and spirited moments. It is this spirit that we hear in this song.

The slaves came to identify their hopes and prayers for freedom with the high purpose of God. They knew themselves to be fighting in two wars; one was their own personal spiritual battle, and the other their common battle for escape from the bonds of slavery. They were consumed by these interlocking passions, and were as enthusiastic about one as the other. In both they knew themselves to be following the generalship of almighty God. When they sang, "I'm noways weary, and I'm no ways tired," they were expressing their certainty that both victories would be theirs.

The slave singers had found that true dedication to the service of God is always stimulating and refreshing. They came to share in that beautiful spirit of Paul, the greatest follower of Christ, who, while sitting in a Roman prison with life's earthly road seemingly coming to an end, surveyed vistas ahead and declared that his greatest determination was to "press on." For him life offered more and more, even as its human possibilities become less and less.

The slaves could sing "I'm noways weary and I'm noways tired, hallelujah," because they were possessed by an inner assurance that life, for them and especially for their children, would surely be better further on. They were like John

132

Bunyan's pilgrim, who when asked where he was going always answered with positive assurance, "I'm going to Mount Zion." The humble slaves knew in their hearts that they were going on to a far more glorious day. Though ever surrounded by the darkness of slavery they caught glimpses of the distant dawn. So they could cheer one another along as they shouted:

> Members, don't git weary, members, don't git
>   weary,
> Keep yo' lamp trimmed an' a-burnin', keep yo' lamp
>   trimmed an' a-burnin',
> For de work's mos' done.

"I'm noways weary and I'm noways tired, hallelujah," sang the unwearied slaves; "I expect to shout 'O glory' when de world's on fire. / O glory, hallelujah!"

Balm in Gilead

There is a balm in Gilead,
　　To make the wounded whole;
There is a balm in Gilead,
　　To heal the sin-sick soul.

Sometimes I feel discouraged
　　And think my work's in vain,
But then the Holy Spirit
　　Revives my soul again.

If you cannot preach like Peter,
　　If you cannot pray like Paul,
You can tell the love of Jesus,
　　And say he died for all.

Is there no balm in Gilead; is there no physician there? why then is not the health of the daughter of my people recovered?—Jeremiah 8:22

Jeremiah, the great prophet of the sorrowful heart and the possessor of the rare gift of identifying with the afflictions of others, was brokenhearted because of the seemingly incurable state of his sin-sick people. He knew that there was no balm on earth that could heal sinful souls. He turned to Gilead, where precious balm could be found, and to which physicians often resorted for their medicines. But even here there was no balm for the sin-sick soul. Thus he cried

135

out in despair: Is there no balm in Gilead? is there no physician there?

The lowly singers of the Negro spirituals knew something of this deep heartsickness and soul-weariness of which the great prophets spoke. They not only knew the weariness of sin, but also knew what it meant to be broken and bruised and crushed by the bitter experience of slavery. It was seemingly nothing short of Divine Providence that caused those slaves to misunderstand the famous cry of Jeremiah. Their interpretation of those precious words has proved to be a blessing to man, and has given to him one of his most beautiful songs. While singing out of their own experience, they rendered an answer to this passage rather than asking the question. Jeremiah's cry of despair became through them and for them a song of victory and assurance of salvation.

This song is without a doubt one of the most tender and sublime expressions of the Christian faith and hope. It is so simple, so childlike, so pure, and yet so true. Through it the slaves made known that they had found in the Christ of Calvary healing for all their hurts. There surely must well up in the heart of every true follower of Christ a rapturous amen as he listens to those beautiful words of assurance. Let us hear them again:

> Sometimes I feel discouraged
> And think my work's in vain,
> But then the Holy Spirit
> Revives my soul again.

Paul, in his letter to the Romans, put it this way: "Where sin abounded, grace did much more abound." There is indeed a balm in Gilead to heal a sin-sick soul.

I can never forget my first experience of the healing balm of Christ. It happened when I was around five or six years old. I was sent to the country store to make a small purchase for my mother. Not having any money for myself, I contrived a plan whereby I could have some money to buy some candy. Having cut down on my mother's order and bought some candy for myself, I returned home with a foolproof alibi. After my report my father, in disbelief, hastened to the store and quickly discovered that I had not applied all of the money on the items sent for by my mother. When he returned home that evening, fear and dread struck my little heart, but to my surprise I received neither strap nor scolding. Simple and calm words expressed the deep disappointment of my father. I immediately felt a deep sense of alienation from my parents and from God. I was alone in spirit and heavy of heart. For several days I carried a deep and haunting sense of guilt and shame, and could not for the life of me face my parents. I had been inspired to pray all of my life, as my home was surrounded by an atmosphere of prayer. I can never forget that most precious moment when I knelt by the little barn, where I had often seen my father at prayer. I do not know what I said, I only know that in some fashion I prayed and heaven heard my prayer. A light flooded my life, my burden was lifted, my sense of sin and guilt and alienation was gone. I was no longer separated from my parents or from God. I was again truly at home. I had been made whole.

This surely must have been something of what our fore-parents sang about. This forgiveness, this healing, this restoration, all of which are found in the living Christ.

The singers also reminded us that there is a balm in

137

Gilead to make the wounded whole. Surely we cannot ignore their testimony. For we too live in days when there are many open and flowing wounds, many hurts, many reasons for discouragement. We find here as in many of the great spirituals this alternating between the protest element and the religious element. The slaves were saying that they knew what it meant to carry in their souls the deep and unbearable wounds of slavery.

No people were better prepared to speak of Christ's making the wounded whole than those humble and lowly slaves. For they knew what it meant to be wounded in body, mind, and soul. They knew the deep hurt and sorrow of separation from their dearest ones, mother and children. They knew what it meant to be beaten and driven like dumb cattle. They knew what it meant to be stripped of all human dignity, to be alienated and depersonalized. Yet they could proclaim in an uncanny way that they had found in Christ a balm that made whole even such wounded. They share this Christ-given victory with all who are wounded and broken and battered by life today. There is a balm in Gilead to make even the wounded whole.

I Know de Lord Has Laid His Hands on Me

O I know de Lord, I know de Lord,
   I know de Lord has laid his hands on me.
O I know de Lord, I know de Lord,
   I know de Lord has laid his hands on me.

Did eber you see de like befo',
   I know de Lord has laid his hands on me,
King Jesus preachin' to de po'?
   I know de Lord has laid his hands on me.

O wasn't dat a happy day,
   I know de Lord has laid his hands on me,
When Jesus washed my sins away?
   I know de Lord has laid his hands on me.

My Lord has done just what he said,
   I know de Lord has laid his hands on me,
He's healed de sick and raised de dead,
   I know de Lord has laid his hands on me.

At midday, O king, I saw in the way a light from heaven, above the brightness of the sun, shining round about me and them which journeyed with me. And when we were all fallen to the earth, I heard a voice speaking unto me, and saying in the Hebrew tongue, Saul, Saul, why persecutest thou me? it is hard for thee to kick against the pricks. And

139

I said, Who art thou, Lord? And he said, I am Jesus whom thou persecutest. But rise, and stand upon thy feet: for I have appeared unto thee for this purpose, to make thee a minister and a witness both of these things which thou hast seen, and of those things in the which I will appear unto thee.—Acts 26:15-16

At midnight Paul and Silas prayed, and sang praises unto God: . . . and suddenly there was a great earthquake, so that the foundations of the prison were shaken: and immediately all the doors were opened, and every one's bands were loosed.—Acts 16: 25-26

Here is a beautiful expression of the deep humility and religious assurance that often characterized the lives of the Christian slaves. These religious singers knew that the Lord had laid hold on them; they knew that they had been claimed and set apart for the service of their Divine Master. Thus they said, "I know de Lord has laid his hands on me." In this expression of certainty their voices are blended with millions of Christians across the years who have come under the saving influence of our Lord. From Paul to Augustine to Martin Luther to John Wesley to the slaves, a swelling chorus has declared: I know the Lord has laid his hands on me. This sense of having received a personal call characterizes the life and service of every true follower of the Lord. Such a call is sometimes dramatic and flashing, or at other times just a gradual unfolding of God's purpose in one's life. And yet before one can do the Lord's work, he must know something of this vital experience.

It may be that much of the halfhearted and lukewarm

Christianity of our day is due to the absence of this first-hand and vibrant, fresh assurance that one has been really called. Harry Emerson Fosdick said, in his characteristic way, that "It is possible for one to be inoculated with a mild dose of Christianity which may render him immune to the real thing." But not so, the slave singers. They had felt the warm personal touch of a divine hand. They knew that the spirit of the Lord was at work in their lives. They would sing, "O happy day! O happy day!/When Jesus washed my sins away." This is indeed one of the blessed assurances that comes to a believer when Christ's loving hands have been laid upon him. He knows deep down in his own soul that God, for Christ's sake, has forgiven him. An emphasis on personal experience, I feel, was a dominant element in the lives of the Christian slaves. They knew that Christ Jesus had come into the world to save sinners. And whenever his loving hands touch a weary soul even today, there is always that blessed "Go in peace and sin no more."

My early childhood days were often spent near the altar and in the midst of the deep religious fervor of some of the former slaves and their children. I can never forget those wonderful highly emotional seasons of worship; the shouting of a forgiven soul and the thanksgiving praises for the living presence of Christ in their midst. They would often sing for the sake of the sinner the words of blessed assurance, "I know de Lord will hear you pray, / For he heard me pray, 'long time ago."

My grandfather used to tell with great joy of his first-hand experience of the loving forgiveness of God. He would tell his experience shedding tears of radiant joy. He told how as a lad he sorrowfully sought the Lord and was found by the Lord; and how the Lord gently and kindly laid his

141

hands upon him. He would say that because of that wonderful experience, the morning was indeed brighter, his heart gloriously lighter, the birds song sweeter. Yes, everything around him seemed to be swinging in perfect rhythm to the tune of the lovely song of deliverance which had come to him, "O I know the Lord has laid his hands on me."

This lovely song of the slaves is not only a joyful testimony to the forgiveness of sin, but also a bold and happy witness to the redirection of their lives. They knew that when the hands of God, lay hold upon them, their lives had been redirected. They knew themselves to be lured by new affections. They could sing triumphantly,

> Things I used to do I don't do any more;
>   Things I used to love I don't love anymore;
> Fears I used to hold I don't hold anymore;
>   There's a great change in my life since
>   I've been reborn.

Take this joyful and triumphant note from the stream of Christian history, and Christian history would be void of its sweetest song. Take from Christian tradition this testimony of the rechanneling and redirection of lives, and Christianity would become weak and impotent. But leave it there, and Paul's testimony makes sense. "But what things were gain to me, those I counted loss for Christ. Yea doubtless, and I count all things but loss for the excellency of the knowledge of Christ Jesus my Lord." Perhaps there is nothing that our own weak and insipid brand of Christianity needs more than the fresh assurance and warm and enthusiastic witness on the part of the followers of Christ that

142

the Lord has indeed laid his hands upon them. Here the slave's song speaks to us with a great sense of urgency.

Those singers were assured also that in the laying on of the Lord's hands they had found a new master, rather a new master had found them and laid his special claim upon them. In his service they had found not burden, and misery, and fear, but freedom and joy and peace. So real, so vital, and so personal was this new relationship with Christ that they could sing, "Did you ever see de like befo', King Jesus preaching to de po'." Yes, King Jesus had come—even to the poor slaves—preaching deliverance to the captives.

Finally, those unknown singers could say "I know the Lord has laid his hands on me," because they had experienced in their hearts what John Wesley so often called the inner witness. They would remind us that there is something within us akin to our Lord, "Something within me just holdeth the reins, something's within me that banishes pain." This expression seems to sum up their testimony which declared they wanted to be more like him. It must be remembered that they always placed great store upon a religion that could be felt, "Yes, God is real, for I can feel him in my soul." They could say, "I felt like shouting when I told Jesus to write my name, I felt like shouting when I told Jesus to write my name, I felt mighty happy when I told Jesus to write my name, I loved everybody when I told Jesus to write my name." An elderly lady put this matter of heartfelt religion in this manner: "If you ain't seen nothing, if you ain't heard nothing, and if you ain't felt nothing, then you ain't got nothing." To the slaves, religion was dramatic and dynamic; theirs was no dry-as-dust religion. They often described their experience with God by saying their spiritual dungeon had been shaken

143

and the chains and shackles had fallen off. They knew that their God had spoken for them saying, "Loose him and let him go."

They surely were in line with the thinking of Paul when they spoke of the inner witness of the Spirit. "The Spirit itself beareth witness with our spirit, that we are the children of God: And if children, then heirs; heirs of God, and joint-heirs with Christ; if so be that we suffer with him, that we may be also glorified together." (Romans 8:16-17.)